Punch Happy

Punch Art Secrets for Scrapbooks and Gifts

Tracey L. Isidro

with Souzzann Y.H. Carroll

Living Vision Press
Bountiful, Utah

ISBN 0-9663318-1-8

Living Vision Press
P.O. Box 326
Bountiful, UT 84011

Table of Contents

Dedication

This honor belongs to the Almighty Creator himself, God. Without him, we are nothing. Thanks to him for allowing me to enjoy a very small taste of what it's like to create something. I would also like to dedicate this very first book to the two most important people in my life, because without them, I wouldn't be where I am today: Thanks so much to my mother and father, Bonnie M. and Cyril J. Nipper, for choosing to be my parents, for their love and guidance throughout my life. I love you both.

Acknowledgements

Special appreciation goes to my loving husband of 17 years, Freddy, who puts up with my endless chatter and my two sons, Victor and Andres, who are growing into fine young men ever so quickly. I'm so proud of you both. All three of you are my very life, and I wouldn't trade you for any other.

A very special thanks to Souzzann Carroll who has been with me every step of the way. She provided the strength and encouragement I needed to make this dream a reality. She shares my desire for perfection in presenting these designs to you, and I'm so glad to have her in my corner. Not only has she been my emotional support, she has been the backbone of the not-so-fun technical aspects of this book such as typesetting and illustration lay-out. I certainly couldn't have done it without her.

Warm thanks and applause to all my Internet friends who have supported and encouraged me to get this book done . . . quickly. Many have unhesitantly asked, book unseen, "Where do we send the money?" Special thanks to Amy, my self-proclaimed #1 Fan; to Rachel and Alice, who sent me paper and punched shapes so I could play to my heart's content; to Gloria (a.k.a. "gg"), who dubbed me "Punch Queen Extraordinaire;" and to Linda, who made me laugh with each and every e-mail message she sent - in purple no less!

Many thanks to Kathryn of the Scrap Happy website for placing my ideas and designs on her site for all to enjoy. I could never list all of you but I'm sure you know who you are. You guys were my test audience and what a great group you've been. Thanks so much.

Many thanks to my editor, Jennifer Alves. I hope I didn't make her job too difficult.

Introduction

Do you remember making shadow puppets on the wall? How about stretching out in a grassy meadow looking up at the sky to find an elephant or perhaps a pirate's ship among the cloud formations? What fun it was! Now, imagine a world where you can combine an egg and a tulip and come up with a string of Christmas lights, or combine a star, crescent moon, and a balloon to create a goldfish! "How can this be done?" you ask. "Is it magic?" Well, not exactly, but you do become a magician of sorts when you join the fun and begin on a wonderful, creative adventure with paper punch art.

I imagine some of you have already flipped through the pages of this book and are saying to yourselves that you could never do these designs. You may not classify yourself as the creative type; perhaps you don't even think you can draw a straight line. Well, you don't have to be creative to accomplish these designs! You won't even have to draw a straight line. The only "skill" you need is the ability to read. This craft depends a great deal on visual instructions so I have included a lot of illustrations and photos along with the step-by-step instructions. I believe that anyone who is able to read will be able to create any of these designs with no problem. All age groups should find this book useful. These ideas can be used on scrapbook pages, cards, bookmarks, magnets, and almost any paper craft item you choose to make.

I want to close this introduction with a story about my discovery that designs surround us in our everyday lives and expand our creativity. One of the assignments in a design class of mine in college was to draw an object and then take it through a sort of metamorphosis (by drawing a series of pictures showing the slight changes in each step) which would reveal a completely different object in the final drawing. At the time, I was certain that I could never do something so outrageous. I had no idea where to begin. True to my procrastinating nature, I put this project off as long as I could, until one night while getting ready to shower, I picked up my razor and noticed what a neat design the handle had. It had a graceful curve to it (the manufacturer said this was for "shaving comfort." What did they know?). While looking at it, I suddenly had an idea. I realized the razor had a shape very similar to the broom vacuum in the closet. I guess I should have written to the manufacturers of that razor to thank them for helping me get an "A" in that class with the help of their wonderfully designed product.

So you see, designs are everywhere, and by being just a little observant, you will start finding "hidden" objects lurking about, not only in the clouds and in your shadows, but in places where you least expect them. As you work with punches, think of the little shapes you punch out as shadows without details. Turn them upside down, sideways, cut a piece off here or there, join them together, overlap them, punch them from a color that isn't "normal" for that shape (for example, a gray apple can become a face for a kitten). Don't be afraid to use that imagination you had when you were a kid. You still have it!

Chapter 1

Getting Started

First of all, let me explain a little about paper punches. These tools are miniature versions of a die cut machine. For those of you who are not familiar with what a die is, it is a tool that is used for molding, stamping, or cutting a raw material such as metal, clay, leather, fabric, or in this situation, paper, into a particular shape. In Chapter 14, you will learn how to create more projects by cutting materials other than paper.

All you need to get started is some paper, a few paper punches, an adhesive, tweezers, and plain scissors. Expand your choices and get some stunning results just by adding optional equipment such as decorative-edge scissors, a paper cutter or rotary blade cutter with interchangeable decorative blades, a paper corrugator, pens, or stencils.

Don't think you have to run out and buy every paper punch in sight! I hope to help you decide which punches give you the best value for your investment. My first design ideas came from punches I already owned. I started experimenting with my punches some time ago, because I thought there should be more uses for these tools than just punching out the shape and gluing it on paper. I was reluctant to put a lot of money into paper punches at first. I had the same reluctance about buying rubber stamps. I thought punches were a little restrictive in their uses. Eventually I bought a few. Then I bought some more and now I'm glad I did because I have discovered so many uses for them. Using them is quick and easy; they cut very precise, sharp images, and they're just plain fun!

As I said previously, I began making designs with punches that I already owned. After a while, I started noticing other punches in stores and catalogs that sparked other ideas, so I started buying more and more. Please think of the information in this book as a resource to help you multiply the uses of the punches you might already have. If you are "in the market" for more punches, this book can guide you in purchasing punches that are versatile, worthwhile investments.

There will be a few designs or ideas in this book that won't be "usable" for you, or may not even appeal to you. That is where your own creativity will come in handy, because you have the power to adapt these designs for your own purposes. In the General Directions section of Chapter 2, I describe which punches are easily interchanged with each other. Sometimes, I list as "optional" a punch that isn't absolutely necessary to complete the design. For example, you don't have to have a micro dot 1/16" punch, because you can draw a dot with a pen. It is, however, nice to have one if you decide to create a "lace-edge" border or if you want to layer shapes and allow the color from the base layer to show through. If you already have it, that's great. Dust it off and get some use out of it. If you don't have it, you can decide if you want to invest in one, or if you can just get by with a substitute. As I mentioned earlier, some shapes are interchangeable. Similar shapes, such as the oval, egg, balloon, and even the circle, can be substituted for one another. You will get a slightly different result, but usually that's fine. You will find that many of these designs can be created with only two or three punches; however, more complex ones can require up to ten punches. Start with designs that require punches you already have.

Punch Types

Do you know that you probably already have a paper punch in your "junk drawer" right now? I'm talking about the hand-held punch that makes a dot approximately 1/4" in diameter and is commonly used to make holes in paper to be placed in three-ring binders. (Go check. I'll wait!) These are very inexpensive and can sometimes be found for less than a dollar at a discount store in the office supplies department. Another size that is fairly easy to find is the 1/8" hole punch. There are several companies that manufacture paper punches, including Fiskars, Marvy-Uchida, McGill, and Family Treasures. They come in many different shapes, sizes, and styles. You will notice, however, that not all shapes are created equal. The maple leaf punch from one company looks different than the maple leaf punch of another company. The maple leaf by Family Treasures looks realistic, whereas the ones from some other companies look more stylized like the leaf on the Canadian flag. That is not to say that the leaf on the flag doesn't look realistic; it is just more symmetrical than leaves found in nature. If you use a punch of the same object made by a different company, you may get a wide variation in design and you may not be able to use it successfully to produce what you want. To help you find the correct shape and size of the punches used in this book, I have created a Punch Shapes Reference Key found on page 75. This shows the images of each shape and the actual size for easy matching with available punches. For precise recreation of the designs, use a punch just like the one listed and referenced in the key.

Some punches have handles and are used like pliers and others sit on the tabletop and have a button to push with the heel of your hand. There are small punches that create shapes approximately 1/2" wide, medium punches that create shapes approximately 3/4" wide and jumbo or large punches that cut shapes varying in size between 1" and 1 1/4". Other types of punches are as follows:

- mini (approximately 1/4" size shapes)
- edge and border (punches shapes along the edge of the paper)
- corner rounder (several designs from basic curve to very lacy)
- lace corner punch (rounds the corner in a fancy line and punches out a design such as a fleur de lis)
- decorative corner punch (adds designs along the corner of your photo or paper, usually in a "V" pattern of five shapes)
- silhouette (punches a circle, scallop, or rectangle but leaves a design inside attached to the outline shape)
- double silhouette (same as a silhouette but with more detail such as the word "love" punched from a heart enclosed in a circle)
- extension (long-reaching punches that punch out a shape further in on your paper)
- two-in-one mini (has two shapes, side by side, in one punch assembly)

- triple (three of the same shape lined up in a row)
- triangle (triangular punch with a different shape at each point)

These punches can be ordered through mail order sources listed in the Resources appendix and can be found in many craft, rubber stamp, and stationery shops and sometimes in discount and teacher supply stores. They are an inexpensive and worthwhile investment. Particularly versatile shapes are discussed in Chapter 4.

Paper

Now for more information about the other supplies you'll need to create punch art. First of all, the type of paper you use is important. If you are going to create a design, whether it is for crafts, cards, or photo scrapbooks, you want it to last and stay beautiful. In order to accomplish this, you should use acid-free and lignin-free papers. Almost anyone who creates photo scrapbooks can tell you what those terms mean, but for those of you who haven't caught "scrapbook fever" yet, I will let you in on the secret. For the paper crafter or scrapbook maker, "acid" is probably the worst four-letter word of all time! Acid is present in our environment and can migrate from other materials - even from our hands - onto our photos and paper products, and in time will cause the paper to weaken and become brown and brittle. Some types of paper that are full of acid are newspaper, cardboard, common construction paper, and some recycled papers. I recommend that you do not use these types of paper in your scrapbooks or in other types of crafts. Lignin is also a natural substance that is found in wood and plants and turns brown in time. It breaks down into acids/peroxides and damages your handiwork. Once again, the best type of paper for paper punching is cardstock that is free of acid and lignin. This paper is available in a variety of thicknesses (weights) and colors. I like to use medium to heavy weight mounting papers. The medium weight is sometimes referred to as "index," and the heavy weight I use is the 65 lb. cover stock. Both of these are thick enough to give a nice polished look but not heavy enough to be too thick for punching. I try to stay away from paper that is too thin, such as the light weight 20-24 lb. bond paper (commonly know as regular copy paper) because some adhesives have a tendency to wrinkle these papers and give them a "lumpy" look. To add a little extra flair to some creations, try using printed or textured papers. I suggest that you use paper with a small to very tiny print since the punched-out shapes are fairly small. If you use too large a print, it will detract from your design instead of enhancing it. These papers can be found anywhere that scrapbook supplies are sold and come in a large variety of colors and designs, including polka dots, checks, tiny hearts, and others.

Adhesives

Next to consider is what types of adhesives are available for your paper designs. There are many products available, and you may decide to use more than one type depending on the size and shape of the design, the amount of layering required, and the nature of the project (card, scrapbook page, etc.). The product I use most is the common glue stick. These sticks are not messy or runny like liquid glues, so there is less of a chance of having the paper wrinkle or buckle. Make sure to use an archival quality, photo-safe gluestick for long-lasting results. I primarily use UHU and Avery brands. Other products available are glue pens, double-sided photo tape, mounting tabs, tape runners, and thick glues such as API's Crafter's Pick, Memory Mount and Grandmother Stover's. All of these are long-lasting and reliable for mounting paper products to other paper. I suggest you try several methods to see what you like best.

Additional Tools

One tool I can't live without is my pair of tweezers. Mine are the long-handled ones that have tips bent at an angle. These are similar to the ones used for stamp collecting or for scientific projects. These allow you to keep a good grip on small paper pieces and make your progress much easier.

You will need a sharp pair of regular scissors. Small ones are easier to work with. I also use a craft knife, commonly sold under the brand name X-Acto, with a self-healing mat to protect my work surface, but it takes a little practice to handle the knife correctly.

Optional Extras

Decorative Scissors

Now that you know which supplies are required, consider these additional supplies that provide a variety of effects. There are decorative scissors that cut unique edges on paper to create borders, frames, etc. They can be used to change the look of a punched shape as will be illustrated in a few of the designs such as the pineapple and the bee.

Circle Cutter

A circle cutter is a handy tool that allows you to cut perfect circles in sizes ranging from approximately 2" to a little more than 7" in diameter very quickly and easily. Several types of circle cutters are on the market but choose one that doesn't create a hole in the center of your circle.

Paper Cutters and Trimmers

A paper cutter is useful for cutting perfect, straight lines quickly and easily, and is so useful that I am tempted to put it on the "must-have" supply list. There are mini-trimmers that have a handle which lifts up and is lowered in a chopping motion to cut the paper. There are also several types of rotary blade paper trimmers. Most of these have a round, razor sharp blade which fits in a plastic casing which is slid along a track to cut paper. The Fiskars brand trimmer is unique, because various decorative blades can be used and easily interchanged for cutting beautiful edges on your papers. Another product by Fiskars is the Personal Paper Trimmer. These are very lightweight and portable. They have holes along the side so they can be placed in a three-ring binder and a replaceable blade carriage which slides along a track to cut paper. These are available in two sizes, an 8 1/2" and a 12" cutting length.

Paper Corrugator

Another useful tool is a paper corrugator or paper crimper. This tool started out as an item that many painters and artists had in their toolboxes. These weren't used for paper, though; they were used on paint tubes to squeeze out the last bit of paint. You may have seen similar items on toothpaste tubes. They have "jaws" which open to allow you to place a piece of paper inside the corrugator. You then close the device and turn a knob that moves the paper through two rollers similar to an old-time wringer washer. Each of the rollers has ridges which crimp the paper giving it a rippled effect much like corrugated cardboard. Although you can run punched shapes through the corrugator, it is easier to run the paper through first and then punch out the shapes. This process adds dimension and texture to your projects.

Pens

Pigment ink pens are permanent, waterproof, and will not fade or smear when dry. They are acid-free and come in a variety of colors, tip sizes, and styles, including calligraphy, brush, and scroll types. Opaque and metallic pens are useful for writing and drawing on darker colored papers. Micron Sakura, Zig Memory System, and Marvy Memory brands are well-known, very trustworthy, and versatile for using with paper designs.

Stencils

Stencils of all types, especially those used for quilting, are useful for creating borders and designs for your projects and scrapbook album pages. The paper punch-outs can then be added to the stenciled designs as coordinated embellishments. This is an inexpensive but very effective technique.

Chapter 2

Tips and Techniques

In this chapter I discuss various techniques, handy tips to save time and money, ways to keep your punches in tip-top shape, and pointers on storing and organizing your growing punch collection. First of all, as with any tool, take excellent care of it so it will last for many years. Fortunately, paper punches don't require a lot of maintenance. No monthly oil changes or frequent tune-ups for these babies! Goes to prove that this hobby isn't as costly as some might believe. Naturally, you will want to keep your punches dry, as they might rust. Make sure the "mechanical" parts are clean. Sometimes bits of paper get caught in the crevices, especially in silhouette punches. Use tweezers or a straight pin to pick out the debris. Avoid dropping them on hard surfaces as you may crack the plastic casing. Some punches tend to be a little "sticky" when first purchased. They tend to "catch" on themselves when pushed down and then don't want to release. Several methods can remedy this situation. One method is to insert one of the following items into your paper punch: a piece of very fine sandpaper, a piece of heavy-duty aluminum foil, a piece of wax paper, or even a piece of cardstock that has been rubbed with a bar of soap (remember how well this works on your sticky drawers?. . .your dresser drawers of course!). Make several punch-outs until the punch seems to be cutting more smoothly. More intricately shaped punches, such as a sun with tiny points at the tips, tend to stick more than simpler shapes, such as a heart or star. Another trick is to tap the underside of the die with the handle end of a pair of tweezers which usually causes it to pop back up. All that is needed at other times is to tap the whole punch on your work surface to get the die to release. Using your punches frequently is a good way to keep them in working order and reduce sticking.

Believe it or not, there is a proper stance for punching paper efficiently. When using the punches with a button on top, it's best to stand next to your work surface and push down with the heel of your hand. It is basically futile to hold these in your hand (as you do with the hand-held punches) while trying to punch through paper. It is helpful to keep a small wooden block, a wooden spoon, a coaster, a cutting board, or any other type of durable object that can be used to place over the button as you are pushing down. This not only helps with those tough punches that sometimes stick, it also protects your hand and keeps it from getting sore.

Punch Organization and Storage

I recommend that you organize your punches in a storage container so you can locate them easily. They'll be ready to use, and you will know which ones you have. If they are organized, you will be more inclined to use them frequently, and knowing which punches you already own will prevent you from buying duplicates. If you only have a few punches, you may think organizing isn't necessary, but now is the time to get them organized before your collection grows (and it will). There are several ways to store your punches. Rectangular plastic containers with compartments and lids that snap shut, commonly sold in craft stores and some sporting goods departments, tend to work well for small collections. They are portable and can be labeled and easily stacked on shelves. The one problem with these containers is that they don't hold larger punches, such as the jumbo size, and some do not have removable dividers to allow you to size the compartments as you like.

Rubber stamp users may choose to store and display their punches as they do their stamps, on narrow shelves. The drawbacks to this method are that the punches can easily be knocked off the shelves (and possibly break) and that they tend to collect dust. Another alternative is to use plastic stackable drawer units, which can be purchased in office supply or discount stores. I suggest you get ones with shallow drawers, as you will only store the punches in a single layer; a deep drawer is just wasted space. A deep drawer turns into a bottomless pit with your punches in a jumble at the bottom. Not exactly easy access and digging around can be hard on your manicure as well. Some of these units are on wheels, so you can roll them to your work area or the drawers can be taken out and carried to your work area.

My personal favorite is a unit I found in the hardware department of a discount store. It is made by the Contico Manufacturing Company and is called "Tuff Parts Organizer." It is made from a heavy-duty plastic that won't crack easily. This cabinet has four rows of drawers and a handle at the top with a recessed area just below the handle. This area is a good place to store scissors, tweezers, a craft knife, glues, portable personal trimmer, and a circle cutter. The top two rows have three "bin-type" drawers, and the lower rows contain similar, larger drawers. The smaller drawers can each hold six or seven small punches and the larger drawers are perfect for the medium and jumbo size punches, as well as the round ones made by Fiskars. Each row has a clear plastic door that runs across the front of the cabinet (the doors lift up from the bottom) and can be "locked" into place to prevent the drawers from sliding forward. These doors will keep out dust, but can easily be removed if you don't want them. Not only is this unit portable, but it also has holes on the back for mounting on a work area wall. The drawers can be labeled for easy identification and can be removed as needed to take to your work area instead of transporting the whole unit.

Punch Key

One effective way to keep track of which punches you have is to keep a notebook. I started out with a small memo pad which I carried in my purse with me when I was shopping. I now have my information in a three-ring binder with my other notes. You might choose to keep the small notebook in your purse and a larger version at home for reference as you create punch art designs. Just remember to update both each time you buy a new punch. Punch out a shape with each one of your paper punches and glue them to the pages of a notebook or on a piece of cardstock. If you are keeping a small notebook in your purse, place several punch-outs on each page.

Divide the notebook into sections according to the size of the punches. If you are placing the punch-outs on cardstock, use a separate page for each size of paper punch. I glue them in straight rows across the page and, to keep the pages from looking chaotic, use one color of paper per page rather than using many colors. I also write notes for future reference, such as diameter measurements and any other helpful information about a particular punch, directly below the glued-on shape. I then slide each of these pages into a polypropylene page protector (these are clear, top-loading, inert plastic pockets with holes punched along the side and can be found at most discount or office supply stores) and place them in a three-ring binder.

Handling and Mounting Tips

A trick for working with small paper punch-outs is to use a pair of tweezers to hold and pick them up. My fingers seem to be twice their normal size when I try to pick up these little bits of paper, but when I use tweezers, I have no problem. I usually use glue sticks, so after picking up a paper shape with my tweezers, I place it on the end of the glue stick. After sliding it lightly across the glue until it's sticking over the edge, I grab it again with my tweezers and place it where I want it. I smooth it down with my fingers to make sure it is mounted securely. I generally use glue sticks, but occasionally I use a glue pen or photo tape. The glue pen comes in handy for placing small dots of glue on the backs of shapes, but don't use too much glue or it will seep out when you place the shape on your paper. This creates a mess, and since the glue is liquid, you may end up with wrinkles and "warped" paper. Some of these pens tend to clog and can be frustrating to use. Photo-safe tapes and tape runners are extremely handy but somewhat difficult for use on small pieces. These tapes are sticky on both sides, so you sandwich it between your shape and your page. Some come in refillable dispensers that you roll on the back of the punched item and then apply the piece to your page. Another method is to place photo tabs or a piece of the tape on your paper before punching the shape. After punching the shape from the paper with the tape attached, peel off the backing and place the shape onto your page as usual.

I also like API's Crafter's Pick, Memory Mount glue. This high quality glue with a thick consistency is highly recommended for mounting paper items. It holds very securely, dries clearly, and won't curl, wrinkle, or discolor your papers. You need to apply only a minute amount, using the tip of a toothpick, and if you keep the lid closed tightly when storing the glue, it will last a very long time. I recommend this glue for layering so that all the pieces will be held securely. An easy way to pick up tiny pieces when using this glue is to stick a toothpick in the glue and then touch the wrong side of the punch-out with the toothpick to pick it up. Then you can use your finger or tweezers to take it off the toothpick and place it exactly where you want it.

Some designs are easier to assemble before mounting them onto your page, as you will see in the individual instructions later in this book. Others can be constructed directly on the page, starting with the background or bottom layer first and building up until the design is complete.

General Instructions for Creating Designs

1. To center one cut-out inside another (such as the key design in which the small heart is punched inside the larger heart), punch out the smaller shape first. Make sure to leave enough paper around the hole for the larger shape. Next take the larger punch, turn it upside down, and center it over the hole from the first punch.

2. Punching small shapes (such as the 1/8" and 1/16" dots) from a small punched shapes can be difficult. The shape may get stuck on the dot punch and could even rip when you try to get it off. The easiest way to punch the dots with the hand-held punches is to squeeze the handle very quickly, hold the shape close to where it is being punched, and pull down slightly as you open the handle.

3. If you buy only one pair of decorative scissors, choose the scallop style. These are perfect corner rounders for all the punch shapes and the classic scallop edge is very versatile for decorating designs such as the balloon, ornaments, tea cup, and others.

4. Use an empty tissue box to hold all your waste paper. These boxes are small, sit on the work table, and stay open (which makes it easy to drop in the paper bits).

5. For any of the smaller punched dots, you may substitute a dot drawn in with a pen to make the eye, nose, etc.

6. The following shapes are interchangeable for use in the designs:
   • Leaves - Hearts, balloons, ovals, eggs, strawberries, even the leaves off the tulip punch may be substituted.
   • Suns and snowflakes can sometimes be used interchangeably.
   • Circles, balloons, and apples can be interchanged for some designs such as faces.
   • Squares can be combined to make rectangles and rectangles can be cut in half to make squares. For a larger square, the roof may be cut off of the house punch.

7. In some designs, a punched shape is changed beyond all recognition with a few snips of the scissors. (The baby booties and Chile peppers are good examples of this.) It might seem like it would be just as easy to cut out these designs free-hand. By punching the shape to start, however, you quickly have a basic shape that is just the right size. Then you need only make a few cuts or round some corners (no tracing or drawing required) to finish making the shape you want.

8. Remember you can use some punches to cut portions out of other punched shapes, such as using the mini flower to take "bites" out of cookies.

9. When it is necessary to punch a dot directly on a punched out shape, use a pencil to make a mark where the dot is needed prior to punching it. This provides a guideline for placing the hole puncher. This method also helps when you cut a shape in half or trim a piece with decorative scissors. Carefully draw the line where you want to cut and then slowly follow it with your scissors.

Money Saving Tips

First of all, you use scrap paper most of the time, so you are already being economical and thrifty! Naturally, you should save any scraps of paper. You'll be amazed at how much you can punch from it. Even a piece as small as a quarter can yield quite a few dots or shapes from your hand-held or mini punches. This will prevent you from wasting a whole sheet of paper on only a few shapes. To keep these bits and pieces organized, sort them by color groups, such as all shades of blues together, all reds, and so on, and then place them in clear page protectors or in individual file folders. The page protectors can be placed in three-ring binders, and file folders can be hung in a file tote or other type of file organizer. The pocket hanging folders work best, since they don't allow the small pieces to fall out. When you need a color, check your scrap paper files before using a new piece of paper.

Since the punch can reach only so far into a page, you will find yourself with pieces of paper with images punched out all around the outer edges. For convenience and ease, cut your papers into narrow strips (approximately one to two inches wide) before punching shapes from it. Turn the punch over to see exactly where you are punching, so you don't waste paper by punching too far apart or ruin an image by punching over another punched shape.

One way to quickly and easily cut many narrow, perfectly straight strips of paper approximately 1/4" wide is to use a paper shredder. These strips are great for borders, flower stems, railroad tracks, and many other things.

Swaps and Crops

Many supply swaps are organized on the Internet. One type of swap is for paper punch shapes. This is an excellent way to experiment with a new shape without purchasing the punch. If it doesn't work for you, you won't waste your money buying a punch that you won't use. It's also a good way to get a shape that you need but may only use for one project. Most of these swaps allow you to request certain colors, types of paper, and which shapes you need. Shop around and join a swap that suits your needs. The swaps are also a way to meet great people and get wonderful ideas.

Another way to obtain "free" punch-outs is by attending photo scrapbook crops, workshops, or classes. (A crop is a gathering of "scrappers" to work on their albums and share their tools and supplies.) If you bring your own paper, you may be able to punch quite a few different shapes. Remember to bring your punches so you can share too. Some great ways to store all these pieces until you are ready to use them are in small snack-size zipper bags, plastic film canisters, clear plastic boxes that come with some punches, or even dental floss containers with the wheel and cutter popped out of them.

Chapter 3

Design Basics

Most of you probably didn't major in art, and you may have never studied design or even given it much thought. I won't go into any long, drawn-out explanation of perspective, symmetries, composition, and proportion. Most of the time, you will be able to tell that something about your layout just "doesn't look right." The technical reason, of course, is probably one of those big art words I just mentioned, but I'm going to give you some easy instructions to try. Follow these simple steps and your layouts will look great. You don't even have to know why they work; they just will. First of all, always lay out all the pieces and arrange them in an eye-pleasing design before mounting anything. Take a step back and examine your handiwork. If you like what you see, go ahead and glue it down. If you're not satisfied with it, you may need to eliminate or add some items.

Placement

For eye-pleasing compositions, always place shapes in odd-numbered groupings. For example, arrange groups of three, five, or seven objects. This is especially necessary when creating clusters for the corners of your pages or cards. Vary the positions of each shape in your design. In other words, place items at different levels on the page, instead of having them in a straight line like a picket fence (unless, of course, a picket fence is what you are making). Naturally, in geometric or symmetrical designs, you would place items lined up in a straight pattern. An example of a geometric design that uses this precise arrangement is in Chapter 11.

Flow

Use parts of your design to draw and direct the eye. Arrange objects to create a continuous flow in your pattern. Avoid positioning items all alone or pointing off the page. One way to achieve continuity is to simply overlap the shapes or place them touching each other. Some punch-out shapes have a tendency to draw the eye to the next shape, which also maintains the flow. One such punch is the spiral. The "ribbons" that hang down from the jumbo bow punch, the tail of the cat punch, and the slight curve of the oak and elm leaf punches all help keep the eye moving around your design.

Size and Proportions

Size and proportion are important factors to consider. Many punch shapes work so well together that we need rarely be concerned with proportions. Many of the punch shapes come in at least two sizes (usually medium and small). Naturally you want the size punch that is most appropriate for your design. Sometimes you can get away with slight size discrepancies just by placing the shapes carefully in your arrangement. Every scene has a foreground, a middle ground, and a background. Most people know that objects in the foreground appear larger. For example, you want to make a Halloween scene and you have only the medium size (side profile) of the standing cat, a jumbo circle, and a jumbo house punch. The cat is out of proportion with the moon and the house. . . . or is it? Place the design at the bottom of your page where it will add a Halloween flavor but won't detract from your photos. This is preferable to placing it at the top of the page which gives the impression the objects are hanging there with nothing to ground them. (Some designs such as a string of Christmas lights or a cluster of ornaments are appropriate to "hang" from the top of a page, but most need some foundation.)

Halloween Scene

Lay the jumbo circle (full moon) up in the "sky" (at least halfway up on the page). Punch three houses and cut the chimney off two of them. Cut out the windows with a craft knife and glue the houses in a cluster as shown. Place the house with its chimney still attached on top of the the other two houses. Cut different shades of paper (light and dark) with deckle edge scissors or tear by hand to create a background of lawn and hills on which to place the house. Make a picket fence by punching several rectangles and cutting each one in half vertically. For other embellishments cut punched hearts as shown to create tombstones, use the small apple punched from orange paper for a jack-o-lantern (cut the facial features out with a craft knife or draw them on with a fine black marker), and add small sun punch-outs (cut in half) for clumps of grass.

By cutting cardstock with deckle scissors, you can create tree limbs and mount them on the edge of the scene as if they are in the foreground. Use the small oak leaf punch to make leaves for the branches and to place in front of the fence to look as if they have fallen there. Cut some in half to make them look like they are floating. Glue the cat on top of one of the larger tombstones or somewhere in the grass in front of the fence. The leaves are large in comparison with the house and the fence, but by placing them in front of the fence, you push the fence further back, and the leaves become your foreground since they appear to be closest to you. If you have the small punch of the witch on a broom, place her next to the moon as if she is flying toward and across it (overlap the moon slightly with the witch). See how it works? It's easy to experiment with sizes and shapes of the punches you have and improvise as needed.

Chapter 4
Most Versatile Punches

Even if you don't have plans to expand your punch collection, there are several punches that I recommend everyone have, whether they are a novice or a pro in the paper punching game. I like the medium and jumbo sizes best because they are larger and easier to work with; however, the smaller ones come in handy and will increase your ability to make many different designs. I think the following punches should be in everyone's tool chests:

heart

star

apple

bear (front view)

circle

All the other geometric shapes such as triangles, rectangles, diamonds, ovals, and squares are also extremely useful and versatile.

My rule of thumb is: the more simple the design, the better. Some shapes, such as helicopters and ballerinas, may not be wise purchases since they are limited in their uses. These shapes are so specific that they don't lend themselves to many possibilities, unless you have a daughter who dances or a husband who pilots helicopters. I know many of you will buy certain punches because the shapes are so appealing you just can't resist them. I had to have the little baseball player for this reason (thanks to Lisa, my Internet secret pal, I am now the proud owner of this punch). At first, I thought its uses would be limited because it is small and doesn't lend itself to creating other designs. I do have two baseball players in my family though, and I figured I would use it for several layouts.

I have since come up with a few different ways to use this punch as you will see later in the book. Naturally, I don't want to discourage you from buying punches that you really like, because after all, it is your money. On the other hand, I do like for each and every tool I buy to work "overtime" for me. I want them to do more than what's generally expected from them. Consider this: I now have about 80 paper punches, including several of the hand-held type. There are, however, some I use much more often than the rest. In addition to the "must haves" mentioned earlier in this chapter, they are:

bow	spiral	tulip	balloon (jumbo)
leaves	egg	tree	train
scalloped oval	jumbo bell	birthday cake	scalloped flower

Chapter 5
Quick and Easy Ideas

Rectangles

Present
rectangle - *2 any color, 1 coordinating color*
medium bow - *1 coordinating color*

Trim the single rectangle along the longer edge and glue all three rectangles in a row, standing vertically, with the narrower rectangle in the center. Glue the bow at the top of the present.

Movie Ticket Stub
rectangle - *1 gray*
1/8" dot punch

Trim about 1/4" off one end of the rectangle and punch a half circle at each narrow end with the 1/8" dot punch. Round all four corners with scallop decorative scissors or regular scissors. Write in words and details with a pen.

Firecracker
rectangle - *1 any color, 1 coordinating color*
mini star (optional)
scallop and mini-pinking scissors (optional)

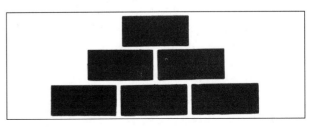

Trim about 1/4" off one end of one of the rectangles using the mini-pinking scissors and punch a star from it. Glue to the larger rectangle. Round the top two corners of the larger rectangle. Draw the fuse with a pen.

Envelopes
(S.W.A.K.)
rectangles - *2 any color*
mini heart punch (optional)

Trim the long edge of one rectangle. Glue the long edges side-by-side with the narrower rectangle at the top. Draw in details with a pen and add the mini heart in the middle of the seam.

(Formal)
rectangle - *1 any color*
1/8" dot punch (optional)

Draw details with a pen and glue 1/8" dot to seal envelope if desired. A star or other mini shape may also be used.

Adhesive Bandage
rectangle - *2 tan (3 if not using square)*
square - *1 tan*

Trim one rectangle into a square, if needed. Trim a little less than 1/4" off the short end of the two rectangles and round two corners on each. Mount one rectangle with the rounded edges out; add the square very close but not touching, and then the other rectangle. Draw dots and details with a pen.

Bricks
rectangle - *reddish brown (as many as needed)*

Start gluing a row of rectangles for the base, add bricks row by row to build a wall, fireplace, ledge, etc. Center each brick over the gap between the bricks in the previous row.

Picket Fence

rectangle - *any color (as many as needed)*

Trim the ends of some rectangles to a triangular shape if desired. Glue a row of vertically placed rectangles for the base of the fence and add a row of horizontal rectangles flush with the tops of the bottom row. Finish with another row of vertical rectangles placed directly above the base row rectangles.

Circles

"8" Ball

jumbo circle - *1 black*
5/8" circle - *1 white*

Write an "8" on the white circle (with a stencil, if desired). Glue the white circle off center on the black circle. Punch jumbo circles in other colors such as red, green, and blue to create additional pool balls.

Bowling Ball

jumbo circle - *1 black*
1/8" dot punch

Punch one jumbo circle in black and use the 1/8" dot punch to make three holes in an upside down triangle formation for the finger holes.

Buttons

jumbo circle
5/8" circle
1/2" circle
1/8" and 1/16" dot punches

You may use only one size circle for your buttons but a variety of sizes looks best (as if someone just poured out the contents of grandma's button box). The jumbo and 5/8" circles look best with 1/8" holes and the 1/2" (or even 1/4") circles look best with 1/16" holes. (See button border illustration in Chapter 11.) To center the holes in your buttons most easily, punch the tiny noles first. Turn the circle punch upside down and center it over the holes before punching out the buttons. Add details with a pen.

Peppermint Candy

jumbo circle - *1 red*
medium snowflake - *1 white*

Glue the snowflake to the center of the circle.

Santa's Cookies

jumbo circle - *1 any color*
5/8" circle - *3 light brown, 3 dark brown*
1/16" dot punch (optional)

With the dot punch, make several holes in each light brown circle in a random pattern and glue these over the dark brown circles. Use the lid of a glue stick or a drafting circle template to draw a smaller circle on the jumbo circle for the plate rim. Write the word "Santa" on the rim with an opaque pen. (If you aren't using the dot punch, draw the chips on the light brown cookies with a pen.) Glue the cookies on the plate, overlapping them in a triangle pattern.

Jingle Bell

jumbo circle - *1 gray*
spiral - *1 gray*
1/4" dot punch

Glue the spiral to the circle as shown. Punch two 1/4" dots in the lower section of the circle. Starting at the bottom edge of the circle, use regular scissors to cut up to each dot as illustrated.

Bears

Babies

medium bear - *1 skin colored, 1 white*
small bow - *any color, 1 for each bonnet (optional)*
small egg - *any color, 1 for each bonnet and bib (optional)*
1/4" dot punch (optional)

Trim the white bear as shown to create a diaper. Trim the ears off the other bear and glue on the diaper, lining up the shape with the bottom bear. Draw the facial features with a pen. To add a bib, use the dot punch to cut a half circle from the narrow tip of an egg. Add details with an opaque pen and glue on the baby's chest. For a baby bonnet, glue an egg behind the head as shown and add a small bow at the neck.

Child in a Bear Suit

medium bear - *1 skin colored, 1 dark brown*
1/4" dot punch

Cut the tips of the arms off of the dark brown bear and use the dot punch to make a hole in the center of the face area. Glue the brown bear over the other bear and draw in the details with a pen.

Character Bear

medium bear - *1 gold, 1 red*

Trim the red bear into a t-shirt shape. Glue the shirt on the gold bear and draw in the details.

Teddy Bear

medium bear - *1 dark brown*
small egg - *1 light brown*
1/8" dot - *1 light brown*
1/4" dot punch

Using the 1/4" dot punch, punch a half circle from the narrow end of the egg. Glue the trimmed egg to the bear's stomach and the dot to his face for his muzzle. Draw stitching and facial details with a pen.

Panda

medium bear - *1 black, 1 white*

Trim the white bear as shown and glue it over the black bear. Draw facial details with a pen.

Gingerbread Man

medium bear - *1 reddish brown*

Trim the ears and toes off as shown. Use an opaque pen to draw the squiggly icing and a black pen to draw buttons and facial features.

Celebration Bears

Valentine Bear - Add a heart as if he were holding it.

Easter Bear - Give the bear a chocolate bunny and pastel egg.

Halloween Bear - On an orange apple, draw a face with a black pen and color the stem brown to give the bear a jack-o-lantern.

Christmas Bear - Punch a square and add a bow for a present.

Birthday Bear - Punch a white birthday cake and draw on candle color, flames, cake decorations, and plate details.

Sunday Best Bear - Give the bear a bow tie.

Beach Bum Bear - Make the bear a beach ball using a 1/2" circle with the segments colored in.

Honey Bear - Make a honey pot from a tan birthday cake. Cut off the candles, turn it upside down, and write the word "honey."

Balloon Bear - Draw two lines with a straight edge in a long narrow "V" shape. Glue a balloon to each and then glue the bear with his hand over the balloon strings. Add details with a pen.

Kite Bear - Punch a diamond and two tulips from the colors of your choice. Trim off the stems and tulip tops. Draw lines vertically and horizontally across the diamond. Draw a long, straight, kite string and a shorter, curly line coming from the top of the long line. Glue the diamond at the top of the straight line and add the leaves to the bottom of the kite and on the kite tail. Glue the bear with his hand over the line.

Cats

Cat and Mouse
Cut a small heart in half and add two 1/8" dots for ears to make a mouse. Draw the tail and other details in with a pen

Cat with Yarn
Punch a ball of yarn from any color that you have a pen to match, using the 1/4" dot punch. Add the yarn string with a matching pen and the cat's features with black.

Halloween Cat
Punch a gold moon with the jumbo circle punch and add a black silhouetted cat.

Cat and Fish Bowl
Make the fish bowl by trimming a thin slice off the top and bottom of a 5/8" circle punched from light blue or gray. Add details with a pen.

Hand Ideas

Hands Applauding
Punch out two hands, one in a darker shade if desired to give contrast and to make the back hand appear further away. Mount the first hand on the page with the thumb pointing up and place the other hand a little lower, overlapping the first one.

Hand with Baseball
Add a baseball made from a 1/2" circle with the stitching details drawn on.

Hand with Yo-Yo
Make the yo-yo with two ovals punched from the color of your choice. Draw a vertical line on your page with a ruler and glue a hand, thumb pointing down, at the top of the line. Draw a loop around the middle finger as if it is tied on. Glue the two ovals at the end of the line with the top oval overlapping the bottom one. Add some motion lines around the yo-yo.

Hands Tying a Bow
Mount two hands and a bow with the thumbs under the bow loops and the index fingers on top.

Garden or Work Gloves
hand - *2 tan or gray, 2 green or blue*
mini-pinking scissors

Trim the straight end of each of the gray or tan hands with mini-pinking scissors and glue them on top of the uncut hands. Trim the sides of each hand as shown and draw in the stitching and details with a pen.

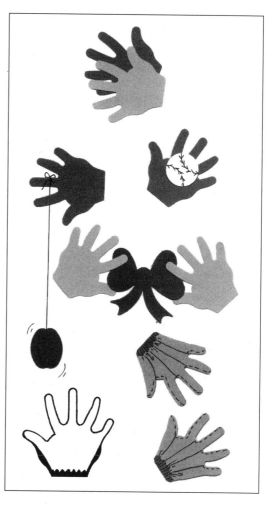

Hand with a Sponge
hand - *1 skin color*
jumbo scallop oval - *1 any color, 1 darker color*
1/4" or 1/8" dot punch

With the 1/4" or 1/8" dot punch, make several holes (overlap them to create uneven shapes instead of perfectly round circles) in the lighter colored oval and glue it on top of the other oval offset slightly so a dark edge shows. Glue the hand, thumb down, on top of the lower section of the ovals with the little finger wrapped around the edge. Mount the hand with sponge on the page and draw in the soap bubbles.

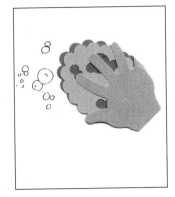

Scrapbook Page Ideas for Hands

1. "He's got the whole world in His hands," for use with photos of Vacation Bible School, Sunday School, or church program.

2. Community projects, gardening, or other work photos with the caption, "Hands to work, Hearts to God."

3. Use a border of hands with photos of the "Hands Across America" or "Hands Across the World" events.

4. Decorate the popular hand print poems with punched hands.

5. "Helping Hands" caption for layouts of volunteer work projects and disaster relief participation.

6. For photos of a person receiving an award, use the hands and the caption, "I've Got to Hand it to You. . .".

7. "Peek-a-boo" or counting game photos.

8. Decorate Fifth Birthday (one hand) and Tenth Birthday (two hands) pages.

9. Photos of finger painting fun. (Add "paint" to the hands with a pen.)

10. Newborn photos with captions such as, "She has feet like her daddy and hands like Aunt Millie!" or "Ten perfect fingers."

11. Use the cloud punch to make a wad of putty and place it in the palm of a punched hand. Use with photos that reveal children are running the show with the caption, "Like putty in my hands!"

12. For wedding or engagement photos, hands holding a piece of rope with a knot in the middle, "We've tied the knot."

13. Use the hands and bow design and the caption, "Time to untie the apron strings," for photos of a child off to kindergarten (or college!) for the first time.

14. Use the hands and bow design mounted over a square photo mat to make a gift package. Caption, "Do not open until Christmas!"

15. Instead of the baseball, use the hand to hold other designs from the other chapters such as a smaller version of the baby rattle with a bow, the flower rattle, a diploma, a baseball cap, or a trophy. Hands can reach for a plate of cookies or the telephone, shake a snow globe, or start to turn on a desk lamp. They can hold coins, marbles, or gum balls made with the 1/8" dot punch or a lollipop made from three different colored spirals with a narrow strip of paper for the stick. Make a toy train (from the medium train punch with cars punched with the medium rectangle) for a hand to push.

16. Make Thanksgiving handprint "turkeys."

17. Remember the other designs in this book that use the hand punch such as the spider, Christmas tree, cherries, reindeer, and clown.

Chapter 6
Holidays and Seasons

Flower Pot and Trowel
jumbo bell - *1 terra cotta*
small star - *1 gray*
medium rectangle - *2 terra cotta, 1 blue*
1/16" dot punch (optional)

Cut the handle pieces from a terra cotta rectangle and a blue rectangle as illustrated, or cut them freehand. Punch a hole in the handle with the dot punch. Trim the bell, rectangle, and star as shown and glue the rectangle to the top of the pot. Assemble the trowel as shown and add details with a pen.

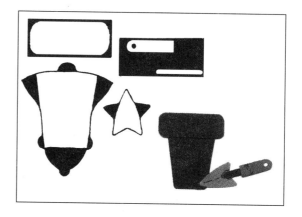

Birdhouses
jumbo house - *1 black, 1 any color*
small house - *2 black, 1 any color*
rectangle - *1 black, 1 any color*
1/4", 1/8", and 1/16" dot punches

Trim the colored houses as shown and trim the chimneys off the black houses. Punch three 1/8" dots in the colored rectangle, glue it to the black one, round the corners, and glue it to the bottom of a trimmed small black house. Punch an 1/8" dot in the small colored house, a 1/4" dot in the large colored house, and a 1/16" dot below the larger dot for a perch. Glue the colored houses on the black houses, make a stand for the large house from strips cut from a black rectangle, and draw on the strings for the small houses.

Beehive
jumbo balloon - *1 brown or gold*
1/4" dot punch
scallop decorative scissors

Trim a sliver off the wider end of the balloon and punch a partial circle in the middle of that end with the dot punch. Use the scalloped scissors to trim right along the edge of the balloon as shown. Draw in bees and details on the hive.

Doghouse
jumbo house - *1 brown, 1 black*
small oval
medium bunny (optional) - *1 dog-colored*

Trim the brown house as shown and use the oval punch to cut a doorway. Trim the round end of the cut out piece flat and turn it over to make the dog dish. Glue the brown house on the black one and add the bunny, trimmed to make a dog, if desired.

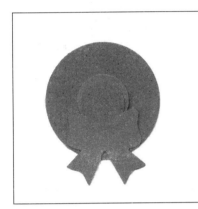

Straw Hat
jumbo circle - *1 gold or brown*
5/8" circle - *1 any color*
1/2" circle - *gold or brown*
bow - *1 any color*

Glue the 1/2" circle on the lower part of the 5/8" circle, mount these in the center of the jumbo circle, and add the bow.

Wind Chimes
small oval - *1 black*
1/4" dot punch - *1 black*
medium rectangle - *2 gray*

Cut the oval and rectangles in half lengthwise and trim the rectangle pieces to make the pipes for the chimes. Draw a straight, vertical line with a bow or loop at the top and glue the oval half just below the bow. Draw short lines on each side of the long line and add the pipes. Glue the black dot at the end of the center line and add motion lines around it.

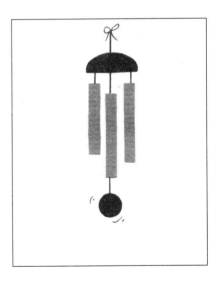

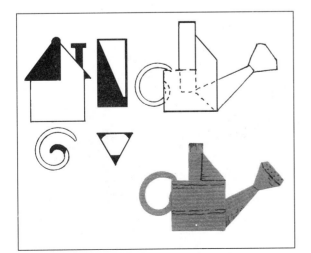

Watering Can
jumbo house - *1 gray*
medium rectangle - *2 gray*
spiral - *1 gray*
small triangle - *1 gray*

Trim the pieces as shown, cut the other rectangle in half lengthwise, and assemble as shown. Draw on details with a pen.

Hot Air Balloon
jumbo circle - *1 any color, 1 coordinating color*
small birthday cake - *1 brown or gold*
mini star (optional)
scallop scissors (optional)
small baseball player (optional) - *1 black*

Trim the candles off the cake and the bat and the feet off the baseball player. Cut one of the circles in half with regular or decorative scissors and use the mini star punch to add a row of stars. Glue the half circle to the whole one. Position the balloon and basket on the page and lightly mark the positions with a pencil. Move the pieces and draw in the balloon lines with a ruler. Glue the trimmed baseball player on the back of the basket, mount the balloon and basket on the page, and add in the lines on the lower part of the balloon and other details with a pen.

Parachute Jumper
jumbo circle - *1 any color*
small baseball player - *2 black*
jumbo scallop flower

Use the jumbo scallop flower (upside down so you can see what you are cutting) to punch the lower section from the circle as shown. Trim the two baseball players as shown and glue the one that still has a head over the other figure. Position the chute and figure, mark the positions, and draw the parachute lines with a pen. Mount the parachute and figure over the lines and add the other details on the parachute.

Shamrock
medium heart - *3 green*
jumbo bow - *1 green*

Cut one of the ribbons off the bow to use as the stem. Glue the three hearts in a triangle with the tips joining at the center and add the stem below them.

Acorn
jumbo balloon - *1 light brown*
jumbo scallop oval - *1 dark brown*
jumbo bow - *1 dark brown*

Trim the balloon and oval as shown, and cut one of the ribbons off the bow to use for the stem. Glue the trimmed oval over the wide end of the balloon and the bow ribbon at the top of the oval.

Pot of Gold

jumbo circle - *1 black*
jumbo bell - *1 black*
spiral - *1 black*
jumbo scallop oval - *1 gold*
1/4" dot punches - *1 black*
1/8" - *several gold*

Trim the circle and bell as shown and glue the bell behind the circle. Cut the oval into three pieces and glue behind the top of the pot to resemble gold pieces piled inside. Glue the 1/8" dots below the pot as if they have fallen out. Trim on the inside end of the spiral and glue it around the pot for a handle. Glue the 1/4" black dot over the end piece of the spiral.

Bat

jumbo circle - *1 black*
5/8" circle - *1 black*
small star - *1 black*
cloud decorative scissors

Cut the jumbo circle in half with regular scissors first and use the decorative scissors on the straight edge of each half to make wing points. Assemble and mount the pieces as shown.

Tombstone

jumbo bell - *1 gray, 1 brown*

Cut the gray bell straight across the bottom and trim off the top tip. Trim the brown bell as shown and glue it over the bottom of the gray trimmed bell. Draw in the details with a pen.

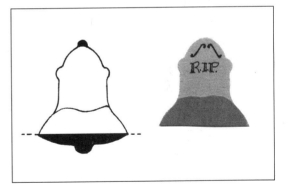

Ghost

jumbo bell - *1 pale blue, 1 black*
jumbo butterfly - *1 pale blue*
1/16" dot punch

Punch the eyes and nose from the pale blue bell and glue it over the black bell. Trim the layered piece as shown in the illustration. Trim the butterfly's lower wings off as shown, turn upside down, and glue behind the ghost for his arms.

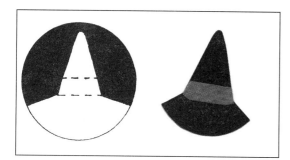

Witch's Hat
jumbo circle - *1 black*

Trim as shown and add a narrow strip of gray paper over the brim as shown.

Jack-O-Lantern
medium apple - *1 brown, 1 orange*

Trim the stem off the orange apple and glue it over the brown apple. Draw in the details with a black pen.

Scarecrow
jumbo balloon - *1 tan, 1 black*
jumbo bell - *1 brown*
jumbo scallop oval - *1 tan*
medium sun - *2 gold*
1/8" dot punch (optional)

With the dot punch, punch the eyes in the tan balloon and glue it to the black balloon. Trim the balloon, the bell, and the scallop as pictured in the illustration. Glue a section of sun to each side of the hat and along the scallop edge of the oval piece as if straw is sticking out. Glue the hat to the narrow end of the balloon and the oval to the wide end. Cut a thin strip of paper for a hat band and add details with a pen.

Easter Eggs
jumbo balloon - *2 coordinating colors for each decorated egg, 1 each for plain, any color*
bunny, bow, mini-scallop flower, all dot punches, and decorative scissors (optional)

Trim the "knotted" end off the balloons to make the eggs. Punch designs in one egg and mount it on an egg of another color. For an all-over design, such as the flowered egg, be sure to punch some partial shapes along the edges. Experiment with different punches and have fun with this one.

Easter Basket and Goodies
jumbo bell - *1 brown*
spiral - *2 brown*
small bow - *1 any color*
small bunny - *1 any color (optional)*
small egg - *1 or more of any colors (optional)*

Trim the bell and spirals as illustrated. Glue the bow at the top of the handle where the two spirals meet. Add the goodies around the basket. This design can also be made into a flower basket.

Christmas Wreath

jumbo maple leaf - *6 bright green, 5 dark green*
small maple leaf - *3 bright green, 3 dark green*
1/8" dot punches - *10 - 12 red*
jumbo bow - *1 red (optional)*

To make arranging the leaves easier, draw a small circle on your page using a drafting template. Cut the stems off all the leaves. Arrange a circle of seven leaves (points toward the center) and glue the remaining four jumbo leaves layered on top of the others with points toward the outer edge. Glue the small leaves here and there to fill in open spaces and add groups of the red dots for berries. Glue the bow to the top of the wreath if desired.

Mittens

medium heart - *2 any color*
small heart - *2 same color*
small bow - *2 coordinating color (optional)*

Cut each medium heart in half as illustrated, glue the small hearts to each trimmed half as shown, and add bows if desired.

Christmas Lights

small egg - *several, any color*
small tulip - *one for each egg, green or gray*

Trim the leaves from all the tulips as shown and glue the wide end of each egg to the pointed edge of each tulip. Glue the lights slightly overlapping each other at the stems of the tulips to resemble a string of lights.

Snowman

jumbo circle - *1 pale blue or gray, one black*
5/8" circle - *1 pale blue or gray, one black*
medium tree - *1 black*
medium sun - *1 orange (optional)*
mini heart - *1 red (optional)*
small bow - *1 any color (optional)*
1/16" and 1/8" dot punches

Punch three 1/8" dots in a row down the center of the gray jumbo circle and two dots with the 1/16" punch in the gray 5/8" circle for eyes. Glue both gray circles on top of the black circles and trim the bottom off the jumbo circle. Trim the tree and sun as shown to make the hat and carrot nose. Glue the hat to the top of the 5/8" circle and the nose just below the eyes. Glue the head to the top round part of the jumbo circle and the bow and heart as shown. Add the mouth "pebbles" and stitching details (if desired) with a pen.

Stocking

jumbo circle - *1 red*
medium rectangle - *1 green*

Trim the stocking cuff from the rectangle and the stocking from the circle as shown. Glue the cuff at the top of the stocking.

Reindeer

jumbo hand - *2 dark brown*
jumbo balloon - *1 tan, 1 black*
small strawberry - *1 dark brown, 2 tan*
medium bow - *1 any color (optional)*
1/4" dot punch - *1 red*
1/8" dot punch

Punch two 1/8" dots in the tan balloon and glue it to the black balloon. Trim the hands and the brown strawberry as shown and glue them to the head for antlers and hair. Glue a tan strawberry to each side of the head for ears, the red dot below the eyes for a nose, the bow at the neckline. Draw the mouth and the details on the ears with a black pen.

Toy Soldier

jumbo bell - *2 black, 1 red*
medium apple - *2 red, 1 black, 1 skin-colored*
small tulip - *1 black, 2 green*
medium snowflake - *1 green (optional)*
1/4" dot punch - *2 red*
1/8" dot punch - *2 green*
1/16" punch

Trim the bells, tulips, and snowflake as shown and trim the stems off the apples. Punch 1/8" dots in the red bell and two 1/16" dots in the skin-colored apple and glue each over its duplicate black shape. Glue the two red apples on each side of the red bell piece to make the soldier's arms, add the green tulip flowers to the shoulders for epaulets, and mount the head to the shoulders. Glue the black bell to the head and add the snowflake piece, a tiny strip of red, and the green dots to finish the hat. Mount the red dots and black tulip leaves on the face.

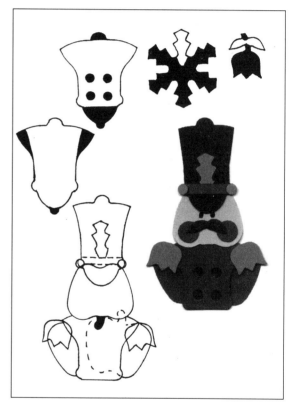

Snow Globe

jumbo circle - *1 pale blue or gray*
small birthday cake - *2 black*
mini star - *2 gold (optional)*
small tree - *2 green (optional)*
small train - *1 dark blue (optional)*

Trim the candles off the top and a tiny sliver off one side of each cake. Butt the two cut sides of the cakes together to make the base and mount them slightly overlapping the jumbo circle. Mount the trees, train, and stars as shown in the completed design (or substitute other shapes such as Santa, ballerina, or tiny house). Use a white opaque pen to make the dots for snow.

Christmas Candle

jumbo circle - *1 tan or gold parchment-like paper*
jumbo oak leaf - *6 green*
medium rectangle - *2 red*
small strawberry - *1 dark gold*
1/8" dot punch - *10-12 red*
1/4" dot punch (optional)

Trim the top off the strawberry and the stems from the oak leaves. Use the 1/4" dot punch to punch a half circle from the top of one of the rectangles, or cut with scissors, and round off the sharp corners. Glue the jumbo circle on the page, add the trimmed rectangle overlapping the circle, and place the other rectangle directly below the first. Glue the trimmed strawberry, narrow tip up, just above the candle and draw in a wick with a black pen. Glue the leaves at the base of the candle with points out and tuck the red berries in here and there, filling in any holes. Hint: Use this same idea as a birthday candle using brightly colored paper and eliminating the leaves.

Christmas Tree

jumbo hand - *15 or more, two colors of green*
medium star - *1 gold*
1/2" circle - *several red*
jumbo house - *1 brown (optional)*

Glue the house on your page for the tree trunk. Mount a row of five hands, fingers pointing down, just above the tree trunk. Work up adding rows of hands with one less hand in each row: five, four, three, etc. Overlap as much as possible and flip some hands so some thumbs point left and some right. Add a few more hands if needed to fill out the tree. Glue the star at the top and tuck red ornaments in where the tree is thin. Hint: Snowflakes, cherubs, bells, bows, bears, stars, and doves may also be used as ornaments.

Ornaments

jumbo circle - *2 for each ornament, any colors*
small tulip - *1 for each ornament, gold or silver*
medium bow - *1 any color (optional)*
mini star (optional)
1/16" dot punch (optional)
decorative scissors (optional)

Punch a row of mini stars across one circle, starting at the center and working out to each edge. Partial shapes punched at the edge make the design appear to go all the way around the ornament. Glue the punched circle over a circle of a different color and glue a trimmed tulip at the top. Add a thin strip of paper for a ribbon hanger, if desired. To make the other ornament, cut a circle in half with decorative scissors and use the dot punch to make a row of dots along the cut edge in the same pattern. Glue the trimmed circle over a whole one of a different color. Add a trimmed tulip, and a bow if desired, to the top as with the first ornament.

Christmas Tree Border

medium star - *as many as needed, any color*
medium tree - *as many as needed, any color*
medium heart - *as many as needed, any color*
medium bear - *as many as needed, any color*
evergreen bough rubber stamp

Make a gingerbread man as described on page 19. Using the stamp of the evergreen bough, stamp various images along the edges of the page. Feel free to overlap or stamp over the outside edges. Draw straight lines from some of the branches in various lengths, and glue the punched shapes at the bottom of each line for ornaments. Draw details with a pen.
tree branch stamp © Northwoods Rubber Stamp, Inc.

Birdhouse Border

jumbo house - *as many as needed, any color*
small house - *as many as needed, any color*
small strawberry - *several green*

Trim the top stems off the strawberries. Using a wavy ruler, draw several lines horizontally on your page, moving the ruler up and over each time, so the lines don't line up directly. With the same pen, draw twigs and branches coming from several places on the wavy lines, and glue some leaves to the ends of some of the branches. Draw straight lines coming down from the branches with a black pen, and glue a birdhouse to the end of each string. Draw veins on the leaves with a pen.

Ribbon Christmas Border

medium star - *as many as needed, any color*
medium tree - *as many as needed, any color*
medium heart - *as many as needed, any color*
medium bear - *as many as needed, any color*

With a calligraphy pen, draw a ribbon across your page. Make sure to curl and vary the design as if it is a ribbon from a package that has just been untied. Make the gingerbread man as described on page 19. Glue the various shapes along the ribbon as desired. Draw stitching details and dots scattered around the shapes with pens.

Layout Notes

For the teddy bear in a mitten layout, make the teddy bear face as described on page 45 and the mittens using the instructions on page 27.

For the Christmas hearth layout, make the Christmas candle from page 29 and the stockings as described on page 27.

circles. p. 18

rectangles, p. 17

hands and cats, p. 20 - 21

bears and babies, p. 19

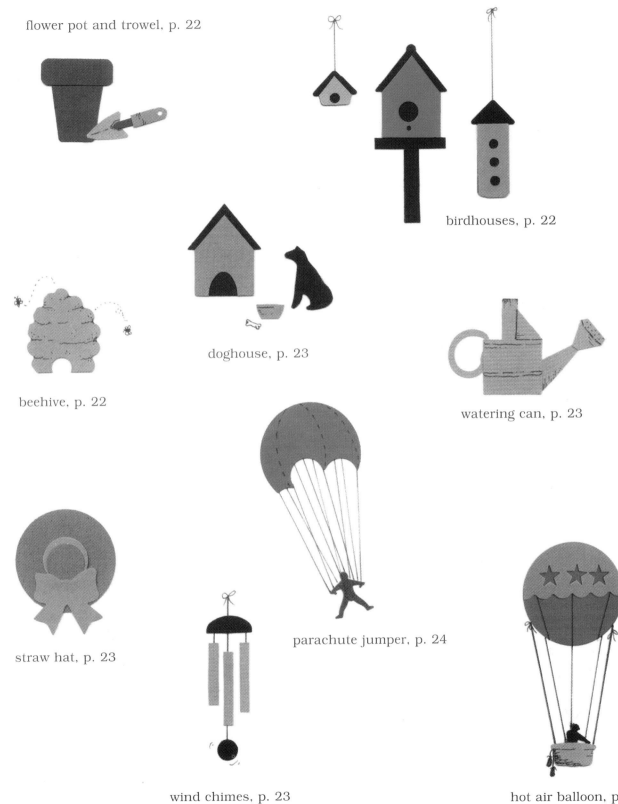

flower pot and trowel, p. 22

birdhouses, p. 22

doghouse, p. 23

beehive, p. 22

watering can, p. 23

straw hat, p. 23

parachute jumper, p. 24

wind chimes, p. 23

hot air balloon, p. 24

Easter eggs, p. 26

Christmas wreath, p. 27

pot of gold, p. 25

Easter basket and goodies, p. 26

shamrock, p. 24

witch's hat, p. 26

scarecrow, p. 26

acorn, p. 24

Jack-o-lantern, p. 26

ghost, p. 25

bat, p. 25

tombstone, p. 25

snowman, p. 27

ornaments, p. 29

Christmas candle, p. 29

Christmas lights, P. 27

toy soldier, p. 28

snow globe, p. 28

reindeer, p. 28

stocking, p. 27

Christmas tree, p. 29

teddy bear face, p. 45

sheriff's badge, p. 45

hobby horse, p. 45

Scrappy the Clown, p. 46

baby bracelet, p. 44

flower rattle, p. 45

rattle, p. 42

pacifier, p. 42

booties, p. 42

baby buggy, p. 43

bib, p. 42

diaper pins, p. 43

gumball machine, p. 43

pull toys, p. 44

ball and jacks, p. 43

Noah's ark, p. 44

wind-up mouse toy, p. 44

pencil, p. 39

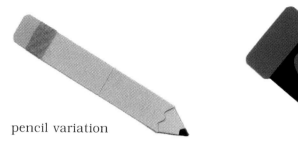

pencil variation

crayon, p. 39

school house, p. 39

mortarboard, p. 40

diploma, p. 40

football helmets, p. 40

baseball hat, p. 40

trophy, p. 41

best of show ribbon, p. 41

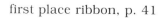

first place ribbon, p. 41

all-stars medal, p 41

Chapter 7
School and Sports

Pencil
medium rectangle - *2 gold, 1 black, 1 gray, 1 pink*
medium evergreen tree - *1 black, 1 tan*
peaks or scallops decorative scissors (optional)

Round the corners of the pink rectangle, trim the tip of the tan tree with the scissors, and glue the tan tree to the black one. Glue the gray rectangle overlapping the edge of the pink one; then glue the black rectangle, with the two gold ones attached on either side, to the gray one. Trim the sides of the tree as shown. Trim the ends of the gold rectangles in a jagged line and glue the tree on.

Crayon
medium rectangle - *2 black, 2 any color*
medium heart - *1 any color*
small oval - *1 any color*

Round the corners of the colored rectangles and trim the edges of the heart. Place the two black rectangles side by side (long edges together) and glue the oval at the center where they meet. Glue one colored rectangle across each end and the heart (with the point facing out) at one end.

School House
jumbo house - *1 red, 1 black*
small house - *1 red, 1 black*
small cloud - *2 green*
small heart - *1 black*
square - *1 black*

Trim the roof off the red jumbo and small houses as shown and glue to the black punched out shapes. Cut a small slice off each cloud to create bushes; trim the square to use for the door and step, and glue them all in place. Cut the heart as shown and glue the larger section above the door for a window and the small one in the bell tower.

Mortarboard
small triangle - *2 black*
small egg - *1 black*
1/4" dot punch

Glue the two triangles end-to-end creating a diamond. Use the 1/4" dot punch to take a "bite" out of the narrow end of the egg (one on each side) then glue the wider end over the seam where the two triangles meet. Draw on a tassel with a pen.

Diploma
medium rectangle - *2 gray or parchment paper*
small bow - *1 black*

Punch two rectangles in gray or parchment paper and one bow in black. Round two edges on each of the rectangles and glue them end-to-end with the rounded edges facing out. Glue the bow across the seam where the ends meet.

Football Helmet

(large)
jumbo circle - *1 any color*
1/8" dot punch
sharp-pointed star - *1 any color (optional)*

Cut the jumbo circle as shown in the diagram and punch a 1/8" dot where the ear flap is. Draw in the face guard with a pen before gluing the helmet to the page. This is easily done by drawing two horizontal lines and joining them with a shorter vertical line toward the front of the helmet. Glue a star on the helmet if desired, or use another jumbo circle as a template for drawing lines along the top of the helmet.

(small)
small baby buggy - *1 any color*
1/16" dot punch

Trim off the wheels and handle as shown and punch a 1/16" dot where the ear flap should be. Draw the face guard with a pen, as described for the large helmet, and use an opaque pen to write a number or draw on a star for decoration.

Baseball Cap
jumbo circle - *1 any color*
1/8" dot punch - *1 same color*

Cut the jumbo circle in half and trim as shown in the illustration. Glue the smaller half at an angle below and behind the upper half as shown. Glue the 1/8" dot at the top for the button. Draw in stitching details with a pen.

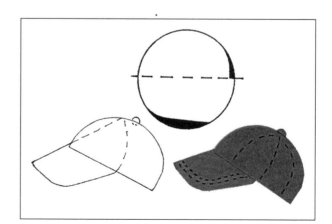

Trophy
medium rectangle - *1 red, 1 gold*
small tree - *1 gold*
small baseball player (may also use ballerina, dog, cat, horse) - *1 gold*
small diamond - *1 gold*
1/4" dot punch - *1 red*

Cut the rectangles as shown and assemble as illustrated.

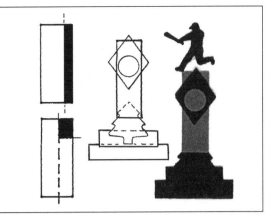

First Place Ribbon
5/8" circle - *1 white*
medium snowflake - *2 blue*
medium rectangle - *2 blue, two red, 2 white*

Glue the two snowflakes together with the white circle in the center. (Hint: It's best to write on the circle before gluing it to the snowflakes.) Glue the rectangles in the following order for each ribbon: place the blue one on the table and glue the white one over it, leaving a little less than 1/4" of the blue showing; then glue the red rectangle over the white, leaving the same amount showing as you did of the blue. Now trim the red edge to make it about the same width as the blue and white stripes. Cut an inverted "V" at the bottom and glue to the snowflakes. (It works best to let the glued ribbon dry a little before cutting to prevent the pieces from sliding.)

Best of Show Blue Ribbon
5/8" circle - *1 blue*
medium bow - *1 blue*

Trim the top off the bow, leaving the ribbons, and glue the circle to the top portion of the ribbons. Write in whatever message you like.

All-Stars Medal
medium heart - *1 red, 1 white, 1 blue*
1/2" circle - *1 gray*
spiral - *1 gray*
medium rectangle - *1 gray*
baseball player - *1 black (optional)*
mini star - *3 blue (optional)*

Glue the baseball player to the circle and trim the legs and excess off. Round the corners on the rectangle and cut the larger portion of the spiral off, leaving just the small curl from the inside. Cut the red and blue hearts in half and then trim another thin slice off one half of each colored heart. Glue them to the white heart, spacing them out as needed. Mount the three mini stars to the rectangle, starting with one in the center, and glue the rectangle to the top of the heart. Glue the spiral to the tip of the heart and the circle below that.

41

Chapter 8
Babies, Kids, and Toys

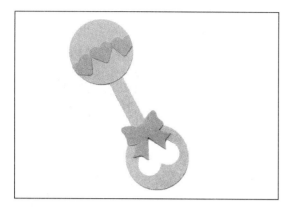

Rattle
jumbo circle - *1 blue*
small heart - *3 pink (optional)*
medium bow - *1 pink*
medium heart - *punch one from blue, center the jumbo circle over the heart-shaped hole and punch out the ring for the handle*

Cut a narrow strip of paper approximately 1/4" wide, in blue, for the handle. Glue one small heart to the center of the uncut circle and then add a heart on each side of the first one. Trim the edge off the hearts so they fit within the circle. Assemble as illustrated.

Booties
jumbo circle - *2 any color*
small bow - *2 coordinating color (optional)*
1/16" dot punch
scallop edge scissors

Trim the two circles as shown. Use the scallop scissors to cut across the top of each bootie. Use the 1/16" dot punch to punch a hole in each scallop to create a lacy crocheted look. Glue a bow to each bootie front, if desired, for more decoration.

Pacifier
jumbo scallop oval - *1 blue*
small oval - *2 tan*
small heart/medium heart - *punch a small heart from blue, center the medium heart over the heart-shaped hole and punch out the ring for the handle*

Trim the scallop oval and one tan oval as shown and assemble the pacifier as illustrated.

Bib
jumbo circle - *1 any color*
small bow - *1 same color*
jumbo scallop oval - *1 coordinating color*
small oval
1/16" dot punch
small running bunny (optional)

Punch each scallop of the oval with the 1/16" dot punch to create a lacy effect. Use the oval punch to punch a half-oval out of the top of the scallop oval and the jumbo circle. Punch a bunny (or other shape) from the center of the scallop oval and glue the oval on the jumbo circle. Trim the edges on the circle around the scalloped edges as shown. Glue the bow at the top edge of the bib with the ribbons touching the tips of the neckline.

Baby Buggy

jumbo circle - *1 dark gray, 1 pink*
1/2" circle - *1 black*
5/8" circle - *1 black*
spiral - *1 dark gray*
small bear - *1 tan (optional)*
scallop scissors

With plain scissors, cut the dark gray jumbo circle from one outer edge to the center. Use the scallop scissors to cut from the top of the circle to the center, meeting the first cut. Cut the pink circle in half with the scallop scissors and glue one half to the back of the gray circle. Add the circles for wheels, the spiral for a handle, and the bear peeking out of the buggy.

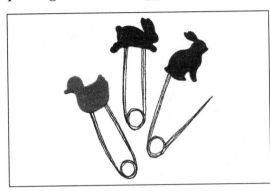

Diaper Pens

small duck, running rabbit, sitting rabbit, train, bear

Punch as many of the above shapes as desired from any colors you like. Lightly draw the metal pin shape (some closed and some open) with a pencil. When you are satisfied with the shape, trace over the drawings with a pen. Glue the punched shapes to the tops of the drawings to complete the pins.

Gum Ball Machine

jumbo circle - *1 light gray or pale blue*
1/2" circle - *1 red*
1/8" dot punch - *1 red, a few dozen in many colors*
jumbo bell - *1 red*
silhouette ornament - *1 black (optional)*

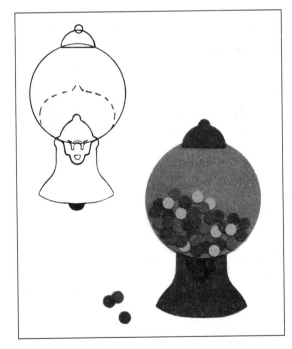

Cut the 1/2" circle in half, glue it to the top of the jumbo circle, and glue the 1/8" dot to the top of the half circle. Trim the clapper off the bell; layer the ornament upside down over the top of the bell and the jumbo circle over the top of the ornament as shown. Spread a thin layer of adhesive over the lower section of the jumbo circle and drop the dots over the adhesive until you have covered the area. Press down to secure them to the page; shake off any loose pieces and fill in any bare spots. Add a few gum balls on the "table" beside the machine. (If you do not have the silhouette ornament punch, draw in the gum ball shoot with a black pen.)

Ball and Jacks

small snowflake - *several gray*
5/8" circle - *1 red*

Arrange the ball and jacks as if they have been used for a game.

Wind-up Mouse Toy
medium heart - *1 gray*
spiral - *1 gray*
small heart - *1 black*
1/8" dot punch - *1 black*
1/4" dot punch - *2 gray*

Cut the gray heart in half as shown and punch a 1/8" dot from each rounded section of the black heart. Trim that heart as shown for the key. Assemble the toy design as illustrated.

Pull Toys
small duck - *1 gold*
medium sitting rabbit - *1 medium brown*
1/8" dot punch - *1 gold, 1 orange, 1 blue*
1/4" dot punch - *2 red, dark brown*
medium rectangle - *1 blue*

Draw two strings on the page. On one, glue the duck, the 1/4" brown dot for a wheel, and two 1/8" dots at the other end for pull beads. Cut the rectangle in half lengthwise, glue the two 1/4" red dots to its lower edge for wheels, and mount the rabbit on top. Glue this to one end of the string and the blue "bead" to the other end. Draw the eyes and string knots on with a pen.
Hint: Make more pull toys with the train, dinosaur, cow, horse, cat, lamb, elephant, pig, and other punches.

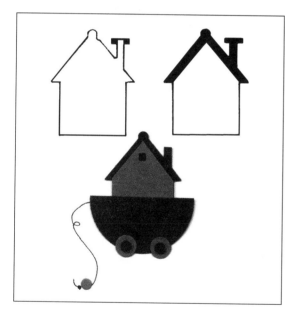

Noah's Ark Toy
jumbo house - *1 light brown, 1 black*
jumbo circle - *1 dark brown*
1/4" dot punch - *2 light brown*
1/8" dot punch - *1 light brown, 2 black*

Cut the circle in half, trim the roof off the brown house, and trim the chimney on the black house as shown. Glue the brown house on top of the black house and glue the layered house to the half circle. Mount the 1/4" dot on the half circle for wheels and add the black dots to the center of each wheel. Draw a string with a pen and glue the 1/8" brown dot at the end. Draw a tiny square window at the top of the house.
Hint: This looks great with two each of the elephant, rhino, lion, kangaroo, and other animals around it.

Baby Bracelet
1/2" circle - *4 pale gray*
1/4" dot punch - *7 blue*
1/8" dot punch - *10 pink*

Write the letters on the gray circles freehand or with a stencil. Lightly draw an oval shape on the page to use as a guideline, arrange the beads on it, and glue them down.

Sheriff's Badge

medium star - *1 gray*
5/8" circle - *1 gray, 1 black*
1/4" dot punch - *5 gray*
mini star

Punch a mini star in the center of the gray 5/8" circle and glue this circle to the black one. Glue these circles to the center of the star and add a 1/4" dot to each of the star's points. Use a black pen to add details.

Flower Rattle

jumbo scallop flower - *1 gold*
5/8" circle - *1 light gray or pale blue*
1/2" circle - *1 red*
1/8" dot punch - *2 red*

Cut a thin strip of light gray or pale blue paper. Glue the 5/8" gray circle to the center of the flower and mount it at one end of the paper strip. Mount the red circle at the other end and the red dots for cheeks. Add features and details with a pen.

Teddy Bear Face

jumbo circle - *1 brown, 1 black*
5/8" circle - *2 brown, 1 tan*
1/4" dot punch - *2 tan*
mini heart - *1 black (optional, may use 1/4" dot)*
medium bow - *any color (optional)*
1/8" dot punch

Glue the 5/8" tan circle to the lower section of the brown jumbo circle and the two 1/4" tan dots to the centers of the 5/8" brown circles. Punch two eyes directly above the muzzle with the 1/8" dot punch, glue the brown jumbo circle over the black one, and attach the ears at the top of the head. Glue a black mini heart at the top of the muzzle (or use half of a 1/4" dot, curved side down). Add the bow at the neck, if desired.

Hobby Horse

jumbo circle - *1 brown*
5/8" dot - *1 brown*
medium sun - *1 tan*
spiral - *1 black*
mini star - *1 tan, 1 dark green*
1/8" dot punch - *2 dark green*

Trim the jumbo circle as shown and cut a long narrow strip of dark green paper. Glue the green star to the center of the 5/8" circle and glue it to one end of the paper strip. Draw the details on the horse's head with a pen. Cut the sun in half and glue each half to the upper portion of the head for a mane. Mount the spiral as shown for reins and add the tan star and two green dots to decorate the bridle.

Scrappy the Clown

jumbo circle - *1 skin color*
jumbo hand - *1 skin color*
jumbo balloon - *5 red, 1 blue, 1 yellow*
jumbo scallop flower - *1 blue, 1 yellow*
spiral - *4 red, 1 black*
small triangle - *3 yellow*
1/2" circle - *3 yellow*
small oval - *1 white*
mini scallop flower - *5 blue*
1/8" dot punch - *2 black*
1/4" dot punch - *3 red*
cloud decorative scissors

Cut a rectangle approximately 1 1/2" by 1 1/4" and a triangle with a base 1" wide and height of about 1 1/4" from red paper. Cut three very narrow strips of black paper for balloon strings. Use a personal trimmer or paper cutter if one is available.

Face

Cut the white oval in half, glue a black 1/8" dot in the bottom corner of each half, and glue the eyes to the mid-section of the jumbo circle. Place a red 1/4" dot below them for a nose and add the trimmed spiral and other two red dots for a mouth.

Hat and Hair

Glue the yellow triangles along the base of the red triangle, add a blue mini flower to the top tip of each triangle and the yellow 1/2" circle to the tip of the red triangle. Glue the hat to the top of the jumbo circle. Attach two red spirals to each side of the head for hair.

Body

Trim the blue jumbo flower as shown, punch a 1/8" dot from the three scallops on one flower half. Use the cloud scissors to trim the other half as shown to make the cuff of the sleeve. Glue the cuff to the wide end of one of the red balloons and glue these to another balloon to make an arm. Attach this whole arm to one side of the rectangle, reaching up. Glue the other two balloons on the other side of the body, as if his arm is behind his back. Mount the remaining blue jumbo flower half over the jumbo yellow flower and place these at the top of the rectangle. Glue the two remaining 1/2" yellow circles below the collar and add blue mini flowers to the center of each. Glue the head just above the collar, slightly tilted as if he is looking up at the balloons.

Hand with Balloons

Glue a balloon to one end of each black strip of paper and glue the other end of each strip to the palm of the hand. Glue the hand at the end of the cuff, bend four fingers down to "grasp" the strings, and finish mounting balloons on the page.

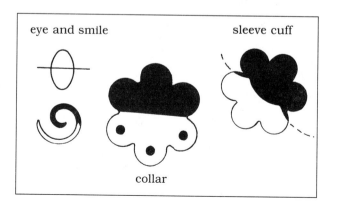

eye and smile · sleeve cuff · collar

Chapter 9
Fruits and Vegetables

Beets
small balloon - *1 purple*
small oak leaves - *3 green*

Glue the leaves sticking out from the wider portion of the balloon. Draw "roots," leaf veins, and details on the balloon with a pen.

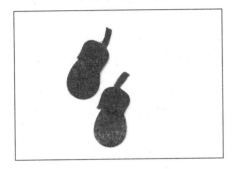

Eggplant
small egg - *several purple*
small tulip - *same number, green*

Trim the leaves from the tulips, turn them upside down and glue to the top narrow part of the eggs. Tilt the egg slightly rather than placing it straight up and down.

Cherries
5/8" circle - *3 red*
jumbo plain leaf - *2 green*
jumbo hand - *1 brown (optional)*

Trim the hand as shown and use it as the stems for the cherries. Finish by gluing the leaves at the top of the stems.

Grapes
5/8" circle - *about 2 dozen purple*
spiral - *3 green*
jumbo maple leaf - *2 green*

Start with the wider end of the bunch (the top) and start layering by overlapping the circles, gradually narrowing down to only one or two grapes across at the tip. Glue the two leaves toward the top and the spirals in various locations as seen in the completed design.

Apple

(whole and slices)
medium apple punch - *1 red, 1 brown*
small strawberry - *2 green*
small oval - *1 red, 1 white*

Trim the stem off the red apple and glue this apple over the brown one. Glue the two strawberries behind the stem with the points up. Draw a reflection mark on the apple with a white opaque pen. Cut the red and white ovals in half and layer the white one over the red, allowing a sliver of the red to show along the edges. Draw in seeds with a pen.

(half apple)
medium heart - *1 red*
small heart - *1 white, 1 green*
1/4" dot punch

Use the 1/4" dot punch to take a "bite" out of the tip of the heart; glue the small white heart to the center of the red heart. Cut the small green heart in half vertically and glue it to the top of the red heart for leaves. Draw in seed details with a pen.

Blueberries

5/8" circle - *1 dark blue for each berry*
small star - *several light blue*
1/8" dot punches - *several brown*
1/4" dot punches

Punch a 1/4" circle from the center of the star. On some of the blueberries, glue on a brown dot or place a star beneath the edge of the circle allowing the points to stick out.

Carrots

medium heart - *1 orange*
small oak leaf - *6 green*
1/8" dot punch

Cut the heart in half and trim as shown. Use the 1/8" dot punch to take a tiny scoop from the top of the carrot. Glue the oak leaves "sprouting" up from the top of the carrot and draw in details with a pen.

Strawberry

jumbo balloon - *1 red*
medium star - *1 green*
spiral - *2 green*
mini scallop flower - *1 white, 1 yellow*
1/8" dot punch (optional)

With the 1/8" dot punch, punch a circle from the center of the white flower, and glue the white over the yellow flower. Trim the balloon and star as shown, and glue the trimmed star at the wider section of the balloon with the two spirals coming out from the bottom for vines. Add the flower over the section where the spirals join. Draw in details with a pen.

Tomatoes
(large tomato)
medium apple - *1 red, 1 brown*
small star - *2 green*
1/8" dot punch

With the 1/8" dot punch, punch a hole in the center of each star. Trim the stem off the red apple, and glue this apple to the brown one. Slip the stars over the stem, and glue them in place. Add details with a white opaque pen.

(cherry tomato)
5/8" circle - *1 red*
small star - *1 green*
1/8" dot punch - *1 brown*

Glue the star to the circle, and the brown dot to the center of the star.

Sweet Peppers
medium apple - *1 red or yellow, 1 green*
mini scallop flower or 1/8" dot punch

Use the mini flower to take a "bite" from the top of the red or yellow apple where the stem is. You can also take several "bites" from the top with the 1/8" dot punch. Glue the red or yellow apple to the green one and trim the sides as shown in the illustration. Add details with a pen.

Chile Peppers
(large)
jumbo circle - *1 red*
medium star - *1 green*

Trim as shown in the illustration and glue the trimmed star to the wider end.

(small)
medium foot - *1 red*
small star - *1 green*

Trim as shown and glue the star to the top of the foot as shown.

Pineapple
jumbo balloon - *1 brown*
jumbo oak leaf - *2 green*
deckle edge scissors

Trim the outer edges of the balloon with the deckle scissors, and trim the leaves with regular scissors as shown. Attach the larger leaf to the narrow tip of the balloon, and the smaller portion of the second leaf to the lower end of balloon. Draw details with a pen.

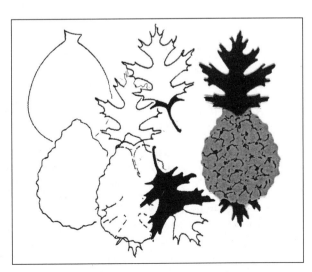

Chapter 10
Around the House

Fishbowl

jumbo circle - *1 light blue or gray*
small balloon - *1 gold*
small crescent moon - *1 gold*
small star - *1 gold*

Cut a slice off the top and bottom of the jumbo circle. The top cut should be bigger than the bottom. Trim the star as shown and assemble as in the illustration. Glue the fish on the bowl and use a pen to draw in the eye, bubbles, and details.

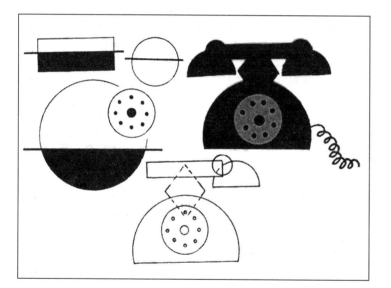

Telephone

jumbo circle - *1 black*
5/8" circle - *1 black, 1 gray or white*
1/4" dot punch - *2 black*
medium rectangle - *1 black*
small diamond - *1 black*
1/8" and 1/16" dot punches (optional)

If using the 1/8" and 1/16" dot punches, start in the center of the white circle and punch the 1/8" dot first. Next, using the 1/16" dot punch, make a hole at the top (twelve o'clock position), and then one each at the six, three, and nine o'clock positions. Fill in with a dot between each of those to create the dial. Draw the circles in the same pattern, if you are using a pen for these details. Trim and assemble the jumbo circle, rectangle, and 5/8" black circle as shown in the illustration. Draw in the coiled phone cord.

Apron

jumbo scallop oval - *1 any color*
jumbo bow - *1 same color*
medium rectangle - *1 coordinating color*
small heart (optional) - *1 coordinating color*
1/16" dot punch (optional)
decorative scissors (optional)

Cut the oval in half and the ribbons off the bow. Trim the heart as shown, cut the rectangle with decorative scissors if desired, and punch each scallop of the oval with the 1/16" dot punch to create a lace effect. Glue the rectangle strip across the top edge of the apron, one bow ribbon on each side, and the pocket on the front. Add stitching with a pen if desired.

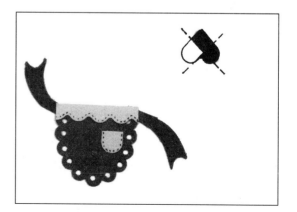

Lipstick
medium rectangle - *2 black*
small oval - *1 red or pink*

Cut approximately 1/4" off one of the rectangles and round two corners off each rectangle. Glue the oval to the untrimmed end of the longer rectangle.

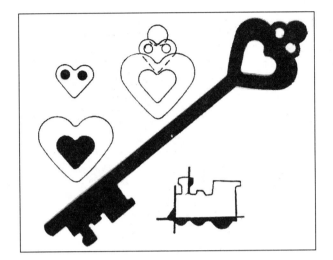

Key
medium train - *1 black*
medium heart - *1 black (see instructions below)*
small heart - *1 black (see instructions below)*
1/4" dot punch- *1 black*
1/8" dot punch

Punch a small heart from black paper, making sure to leave enough paper around the hole to punch a larger heart over it. Save the small heart and punch a 1/8" dot in each of the rounded humps as shown. Punch the larger heart by turning the punch upside down and centering it over the small heart opening in the paper before punching. Cut a long strip of black paper approximately 1/4" wide. Trim the train as shown, round the end of the paper strip, and assemble as shown.

Candlestick
jumbo circle - *1 black*
small oval - *2 black*
1/4" dot - *2 black*
5/8" circle - *1 gold*
medium rectangle - *1 red (optional)*

Cut the top of the jumbo circle off to use as the base of the candlestick, and cut one oval in half. Trim the rectangle to make the candle and taper the end. Assemble as shown. Feel free to mix and match different geometric shapes such as the square, triangle, diamond, and circle as desired. Draw in a flame and wick.

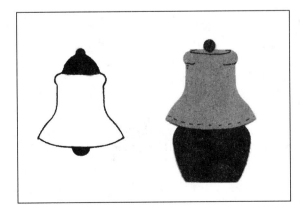

Lamp with Shade
medium apple - *1 any color*
1/8" dot punch - *1 same color*
jumbo bell - *1 lighter color*

Cut a slice off the bottom part of the apple and trim the bell as shown. Assemble and draw in the details.

Desk Lamp
jumbo circle - *1 black*
medium rectangle - *1 black*
medium train - *1 black*
5/8" circle - *1 gray or white*

Cut the jumbo circle in half, trim the train as shown, and round the top corners of the rectangle for the base of the lamp. Use the outer edge of the jumbo circle punch itself to trace the curved line for the lamp's flexible neck. Glue the white circle beneath the jumbo circle half and the train towards the back with the smokestack serving as the light switch.

Pocket Watch
jumbo circle - *1 gold*
1/2" circle - *1 black, 1 gold (punch according to the directions below)*
medium snowflake - *1 black*
1/8" dot punches - *1 white*
1/4" dot punches

Punch a 1/4" dot from gold, center the 1/2" punch over the hole, and punch out the ring for the top of the watch. If desired, you can cut a smaller circle in white by tracing using a drafting template and then cutting by hand. Choose a circle just smaller than the jumbo circle punch. Trim the snowflake as shown for the watch hands and stem and assemble as shown. Use a pen to add details.

Alarm Clock
jumbo circle - *1 gray*
1/2" circle - *1 black*
1/4" dot punches - *2 black*
1/8" dot punches - *2 black, 1 gray*
medium snowflake - *1 black*
spiral - *1 black*

Cut the 1/2" circle in half; trim the spiral and snowflake as shown. Assemble as illustrated and use a pen to draw in details.

Teapot, Cup, and Saucer on a Lace Tablecloth
jumbo balloon - *1 any color*
jumbo bow - *1 same color*
small oval - *1 same color, 1 coordinating color*
spiral - *1 same color*
small birthday cake - *1 same color*
small baby buggy - *1 same color (optional)*
1/4" dot punches - *1 same color*
1/16" dot punch
small tulip - *1 coordinating color (optional)*
mini scallop flower - *1 coordinating color (optional)*
jumbo scallop oval - *2 coordinating color (optional)*

Trim the balloon, bow, oval, tulip, and buggy as shown. Glue the birthday cake to the wider end of the balloon, a bow ribbon to the side for the spout, a spiral for the handle, and an oval at the top of the balloon for the lid. Add the 1/4" dot at the top of the lid for a handle. Glue the flower on the teapot for decoration if desired. Cut each scallop oval in half, punch each scallop with the 1/16" dot to create a lacy edge, and glue the ovals in a row to make the tablecloth. Draw in the steam with a pen.

Teacup
jumbo circle - *1 any color, 1 coordinating color*
small birthday cake - *1 coordinating color*
spiral - *1 any color, 2 black or gray*
decorative edge scissors (optional)

Cut both jumbo circles in half and, if desired, cut the edge of one with the decorative edge scissors and glue it on top of the other half circle. Round the corners, glue the birthday cake to the bottom, trim the spiral and glue it to the side for the handle. Glue the gray spirals above the cup for steam.

Chapter 11
Borders, Frames and Layouts
(Includes Color Illustrations II Section)

Use punches to create borders for your pages, frame your photos or written words, and decorate whole page layouts combining designs from this book. Some ideas use only a few punches while others require several. You may not want to make a border on every page of your photo albums, but borders add so much to the page without making the page too busy or distracting. They work well to group photos and other memorabilia.

There are several ways to frame photos. Some are mat-type styles and others are more complex, such as frames with punch-out shapes arranged in a still-life scene. The easiest and quickest method is to glue a punched out shape at each corner of square photos and mats, or to alternate several different shapes around an oval or circle, such as the running bunny and flower. You can use these techniques with any of your photos, or embellish your titles, captions, dates, and any poetry, stories, histories, and song lyrics with them. The best thing about framing with punch designs is that it is so adaptable and works well in any size.

The page layouts on the following pages will give you some ideas of how to use the designs you're familiar with and how to group them on your pages. By combining smaller designs that would potentially get "lost" on your page if placed alone, you can achieve a scene that matches the theme for that page.

Gift Notes

The bookmark features the inchworm design (now a bookworm) on page 65, the frame is decorated with the trophy from page 41, and the gift tag designs are found on page 40 (mortarboard), 43 (diaper pin), and 27 (mitten).

"He Loves Me" Border
jumbo scallop flower - *3 white*
jumbo bell - *3 brown or terra cotta*
medium rectangle - *3 brown or terra cotta*
small strawberry - *6 green*
1/2" circle - *3 gold*
jumbo hand (optional) - *1 green*

Assemble the flower pots as described on page 22. Cut three very narrow strips of green paper for flower stems, or if you used the hand punch, cut the three longest fingers from the bottom edge of the hand to where each finger separates. Trim the tops off the strawberries and glue two to each of the stems, and glue the stems to each pot. Cut between each petal of the flowers with regular scissors, starting from the dip of each scallop to the center of the flower, but not cutting all the way across. On the first flower, cut one petal completely off; the second flower will have two petals cut off, and so forth. Glue the gold circles to the centers of each flower, and glue the flower to the top of each stem. Scatter the loose petals down below the flower pots. Cut a strip of printed paper and two narrow strips of solid colored paper with decorative scissors, assemble as shown, and write the words with a pen.

pineapple, p. 49

strawberry, p. 48

grapes, p. 47

cherries, p. 47

apple, p. 48

blueberries, p. 48

carrots, p. 48

eggplant, p. 47

tomatoes, p. 49

sweet peppers, p. 49

Chile peppers, p. 49

beet, p. 47

fishbowl, p. 50

telephone, p. 50

apron, p. 50

teapot, p. 53

teacup, p. 53

lipstick, p. 51

pocket watch, p. 52

alarm clock, p. 52

candlestick, p. 51

key, p. 51

desk lamp, p. 52

lamp with shade, p. 51

dragonfly, p. 65

spider, p. 64

ladybug, p. 66

bee, p. 67

inch worm, p. 65

cactus, p. 65

dogwood, p. 65

morning glory, p. 66

daffodil, p. 67

rosebud, p. 66

pansy, p. 67

black-eyed susan, p. 66

sunflower, p. 64

dandelion, p. 64

hollyhock, p. 67

mouse, p. 68

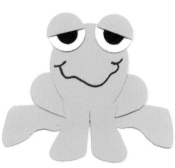

frog, p. 69

bluebird, p. 68

hound dog, p. 69

pig, p. 71

chicken, p. 69

cow, p. 68

lion, p. 70

lamb, p. 70

giraffe, p. 71

monkey, p. 71

Lacy Border Mat

Cut a rectangle or similar shape, using decorative scissors. It is easiest to draw the shape lightly on the back side of the paper first, or if using a template, trace the shape. Using the line as a guide, carefully cut out the shape, being sure to watch where the points or curves of the scissors design touches the line. Using a handheld punch, punch out a series of dots at each scallop or curve to get a lacy effect. Practice on a piece of inexpensive paper first to perfect the look you want.

Make the hound dog from page 69 and add forelegs made with the rectangle punch and paws using the egg punch. The bone is made from a long strip of tan paper and two punched tan hearts. The leash pattern is on page 77. The mat is decorated with the rattle from page 42 and the baby bracelet from page 44.

HAPPY EASTER

Gift and Card Notes

The Easter card and envelope are decorated with Easter eggs from page 26 and green suns cut in half to make the grass. The straw hat design is found on page 23, and the teapot on page 53. The paper clips are embellished with two bears and two flowers. The punched figures are glued back-to-back with a tiny strip of paper, that has been wrapped around the paper clip, enclosed between them.

Spool and Buttons Corner Design
small triangle - *2 brown*
small square - *1 any color*
1/2" circle
1/4" and 1/16" dot punches

Glue a triangle at two ends of the square with the points facing each other and the wider portion of the triangles barely sticking out. Punch a variety of 1/2" and 1/4" circles in corresponding colors for the buttons. Punch two dots in each circle with the 1/16" dot punch. (This is a good time to apply the punch-over-punch technique described in Chapter 2.) Lightly draw an "L" in each corner where the design is going, if you need a guideline.

With a pen that matches the "thread" of each spool, draw a wavy, spiraling line along the "L" and draw a series of smaller spirals and curls coming from this main line, as if there are many pieces of thread scattered about. Glue a spool and several larger buttons in groupings with the smaller buttons scattered randomly along the threads. With a darker marker, draw larger dots at the ends of several of the spirals and many smaller dots in and around the spirals. Draw details on the buttons and spools of thread with a pen.

Ribbons, Heart, and Flower Frame
small and medium heart - *1 each in coordinating colors*
spiral - *2 in a coordinating color*
tiny scallop flower - *3 in a coordinating color*
1/8" and 1/16" dot punches - *several in coordinating colors*

Cut an oval after tracing with a template or use almost any shape. The ribbon banner shape may be cut free-handed or with a template. This type of design looks great in a monochromatic style for a classic, elegant look.

Chapter 12
Flowers and Insects

Sunflower
jumbo circle - *1 brown*
jumbo plain leaf - *4 or more in two shades of green*
small strawberry - *14 gold*

Cut a narrow strip of paper in green for the stem. Glue three of the strawberries on the inside of the jumbo circle with the points facing in and the tops hanging over the edge slightly. Trim the tops of the strawberries even with the edge of the circle. Glue the remaining eleven strawberries around the outer edge of the jumbo circle with points out. Glue the sunflower to the top of the stem and the leaves down the stem.

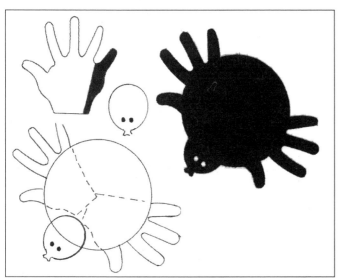

Spider
jumbo circle - *1 black*
jumbo hand - *2 black*
small balloon - *1 black, 1 red or yellow*
1/16" dot punch

Trim both hands as shown and punch eyes from the black balloon with the 1/16" dot punch. Glue the black balloon over the red one and attach one hand to each side of the jumbo circle. Glue the head on the front of the body near the thumbs of the trimmed hands. Draw a web if desired.

Dandelion
medium snowflake - *2 yellow or gray*
small snowflake - *2 yellow or gray*
cloud decorative scissors

Cut a narrow strip and two or three rectangles approximately 1 1/2" by 3/4" from green paper. Glue the two medium snowflakes together in the center, and layer the two smaller ones on top of these. Using the decorative scissors, cut inverted scallops from the rectangles to create the leaves and glue them to the bottom of the narrow strip. Glue the snowflakes to the top.

Inch Worm
5/8" circle - *8 green*
1/4" dot punches - *2 black, 2 white*
spiral - *2 black*
1/8" dot punch

Punch each white dot with the 1/8" dot punch, layer them over the black dots, and glue them to a green circle. Attach the two spirals at the top of the head, and glue each green circle overlapping them one-by-one for the body of the worm. Draw on a smile.

Dragonfly
jumbo balloon - *1 green, 1 turquoise*
spiral - *2 black*
small oval - *2 green, 4 brown*
small egg - *1 green*
small heart - *2 brown*
1/2" circle - *1 brown*

Cut each balloon in half as shown. Glue a spiral on each hump of a brown heart. Mount the 1/2" circle over the heart, and then another heart turned upside down below the circle. Continue by overlapping an egg over the heart, and then add each of the brown ovals to make the rest of the body. Glue the turquoise balloon halves to the tips of the green ovals, the green balloon halves below that, and then glue each assembled wing to the brown heart just below the head.

Cactus
small egg - *6 avocado green*
mini scallop flower - *2 light pink, 1 dark burgundy*
1/8" dot punch

Cut the tip off one of the eggs. Build the cactus by adding additional eggs, overlapping each one with the smaller tip down and the fat end up and out. Punch a dot in one of the light pink flowers with the 1/8" dot punch, layer it over the dark flower, and glue it to the top of the cactus. Attach the other flower so it is sticking out from behind one of the other "branches." Draw in cactus spines with a pen.

Dogwood
jumbo balloon - *4 creme or white, 4 rust or burgundy, 2 green*
1/4" dot punch - *about 1 dozen rust*

Trim the narrow tips of the green balloons to resemble leaves. Using the 1/4" dot punch, punch out a half circle from the wider end of the creme colored balloons. Using the same technique, punch a half circle from each of the rust balloons not quite as deeply as you did on the creme. Glue the creme colored balloons over the rust ones, mount the two leaves on the page, and glue the four balloons in a cross formation overlapping the leaves. Glue the 1/4" dots in the center, covering the opening where the balloons join.

Morning Glory
jumbo circle - *1 blue*
jumbo maple leaf - *1 blue, 3 dark green*
medium sun - *1 white*
small tulip - *3 dark green*
spiral - *several dark green*
small star - *1 dark green*
mini scallop flower - *1 gold*
cloud decorative scissors

Cut around the jumbo circle with the decorative scissors, and trim the maple leaves, tulips, and sun as shown in the illustration. Glue the two outer portions of the blue maple leaf onto the tulips for buds. The middle section of the leaf will be used for the base of the flower and will also be glued onto a tulip. Glue the trimmed sun to the center of the morning glory, add the star, and finally the mini flower. Arrange the flowers according to where you will place them on the page (as a border, corner, or other placement). Add more buds, spirals, and leaves as desired.

Ladybug
jumbo circle - *1 red, 1 black*
spiral - *2 black*
1/4" dot punch

Cut the red circle in half and punch a 1/4" dot on each half. Glue the two spirals on one edge of the black circle, spread apart the red circle halves for the wings, and glue them to the black circle.

Rosebud
small tulip - *several green*
small strawberry - *same number of red*

Trim the leaves off some of the tulips and glue the strawberries upside down onto the tops of the tulips. These work great for a trailing border.

Black-eyed Susan
small oval - *5 yellow*
small egg - *1 dark brown*
medium silhouette tulip - *1 green (optional)*

Glue each oval hanging down from the wider portion of the egg. If you are using the tulip, snip the tiny sections that hold the tulip inside the "frame". Make the stem longer by extending your cut outside of the frame onto the paper to make it as long as is needed. Glue this tulip below the ovals.

Daffodil

jumbo balloon - *5 yellow, 2 green*
jumbo bell - *1 yellow*
mini scallop flower - *1 black*
jumbo scallop oval - *1 yellow*
1/8" dot punch

Trim the balloons and bell as shown. For the mini flower, cut straight across the bottom and use the 1/8" dot punch to create a half circle. Glue the five yellow balloons in a circle with the pointed tips out, mount the scallop oval to the bottom of the bell, and attach it to the center of the petals. Attach leaves as desired and add the mini flower to the center of the scallop oval. Draw in the details.

Pansy

medium apple - *5 gold, 2 burgundy or wine*
small apple - *3 purple*
jumbo plain leaf - *2 green*
mini scallop flower - *1 gold, 1 black*

Trim the tops off of all the apples and arrange them according to the illustration, starting with the five gold apples. Glue the burgundy apples below the gold ones, and the small purple ones at the center of the flower in a triangular formation. Glue the black mini flower to the center of the top small apple, and add the gold one just below it. Glue a leaf to each side of the flower.

Bee

jumbo birch leaf - *1 black, 1 gold*
medium heart - *1 light gray*
small egg - *1 black*
spiral - *2 black*
deckle edge scissors (optional)

Trim the heart, the spiral, and the black leaf as shown, and glue as illustrated in the completed design.

Hollyhock

small strawberry - *5 or more green*
spiral - *3 or more green*
5/8" circles - *4 light red*
1/2" circles - *10 light red*
1/4" dot punches - *4 dark red, 9 light red*
1/8" dot punches - *4 dark red, 5 light red*

Start at the base of the flower, with the larger circles, and build your flower. You will finish at the top with the smallest circles and a spiral. Cut a narrow strip of paper from green for the stem. Use the completed illustration for a guide; however, each flower will be a little different, just as those in nature.

Chapter 13

Animal Kingdom

Cow

jumbo balloon - *1 medium brown, 1 black*
medium apple - *1 light brown*
small strawberry - *1 light brown*
small foot - *2 medium brown*
small crescent moon - *2 black*
1/8" dot punch (optional)

Trim the balloons, apple, strawberry, and feet as shown. Glue the trimmed apple to the wider end of the brown balloon, and punch the eyes and nostrils with the 1/8" dot punch. Attach the brown balloon to the black one, and glue the crescent moons to the top of the head as shown. Add the ears and hair, and draw on the mouth with a pen.

Optional: To make a cowbell, cut a punched medium heart as shown, attach a 1/4" dot for a clapper, and add a bow at the top.

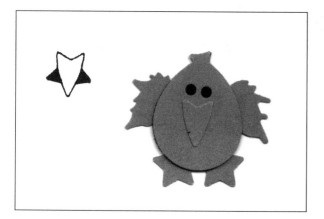

Bluebird

jumbo balloon - *1 blue, 1 black*
jumbo maple leaf - *1 blue*
small star - *3 gold*
1/8" dot punch (optional)

Cut the maple leaf in half vertically, and trim one star as shown. Punch the eyes in the blue balloon only with the 1/8" punch. Glue it to the black balloon and attach one half of the leaf to each side of the balloon. Glue two stars at the lower, wider part of the balloon pointing three of the star's points down. Glue the trimmed star below the eye for the beak.

Mouse

jumbo balloon - *1 gray, 1 black*
5/8" circle - *2 gray*
1/2" circle - *2 pink*
spiral - *1 gray*
small foot - *2 gray*
1/16" dot punch (optional)

Trim the balloons and feet as shown. Use the 1/16" dot punch to make the eyes in the gray balloon and attach it over the black one. Glue the smaller pink circles over the larger gray ones and attach them to the narrow end of the balloon. Add the paws at the wider bottom end and the spiral over to one side. Add facial details with a pen.

Hound Dog
jumbo balloon - *1 light brown, 1 dark brown, 1 black*
medium heart - *1 light brown*
small oval - *1 red*
1/4" dot punch - *1 black*
1/8" dot punch (optional)

Trim the dark brown balloon as shown. Glue the heart upside down over the narrow end of the light brown balloon and the oval behind the "dip" in the heart. Punch the eyes in the light brown balloon with the 1/8" dot punch and attach it to the black balloon. Glue one half of the dark brown balloon to each side of the head for ears, and glue the black 1/4" dot below the eyes for the nose.

Chicken
jumbo balloon - *1 light gray/white, 1 black*
jumbo maple leaf - *1 light gray/white*
medium star - *2 gold*
small star - *1 gold*
small bow (optional) - *1 any color*
medium rectangle - *2 gold*
1/8" dot punch (optional)

Cut the maple leaf and each rectangle in half vertically. Trim the large stars and the small star as shown. Punch eyes with the 1/8" dot punch at the top narrow section of the gray balloon, and attach it to the black balloon. Glue one half of the maple leaf to each side of the balloon; add the trimmed small star below the eyes and the bow below the beak if desired. Glue each section of the rectangle below another to make each leg, and add a star at the end of each leg. You can give the chicken a new "do" by cutting tiny "v"s at the top of the head.

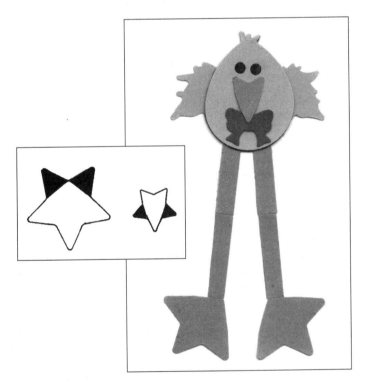

Frog
jumbo balloon - *1 green*
medium foot - *4 green*
medium heart - *1 green*
1/2" circle - *1 green, 2 white*
1/4" dot punch - *2 black*

Trim the feet, heart, balloon, and green circle as shown. Glue the 1/4" black dots to the centers of the white circles and the green half circles over these to create each eye; glue one to each side of the wider part of the balloon. Glue one half of the heart to each side of the narrow bottom of the balloon, and two of the feet below each side of the heart. Trim the top portion of the remaining two feet and attach them to the front of the frog, covering the area where the other pieces overlap. Draw on a mouth.

Lion

jumbo scallop flower - *2 dark brown,*
jumbo balloon - *1 gold, 1 black*
small balloon - *1 red, 2 gold*
small triangle - *1 black*
1/4" dot punch - *2 gold*
1/8" dot punch (optional)

Cut each flower in half as shown. Glue the red balloon at the narrow tip of the gold jumbo balloon, a small gold balloon to each side of the red (in an upside down triangle formation), and the triangle (with the tip pointing down) over the top of these balloons where they all meet. Punch two eyes with the 1/8" dot punch in the gold balloon, just above the nose, and mount it on the black balloon. Glue one half of each flower around the lion's head starting with the top and overlapping slightly where needed. Glue one 1/4" gold dot to each side of the top of the head for ears and draw in details with a pen.

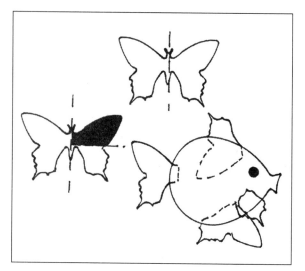

Goldfish

jumbo balloon - *1 gold*
butterfly - *2 gold*

Cut both butterflies in half down the middle of the body section. Then cut one of the halves in half again. Turn the balloon sideways and glue one half of a butterfly at the round end to make a tail. Glue another half at the bottom and a third half butterfly piece at the top of the balloon with the tips pointing toward the tail. Now glue the quarter butterfly piece to the lower part of the balloon on the outside with the point directed down. Make a dot with a black pen for the eye or use the 1/8" dot punch.

Lamb

jumbo circle - *1 dark gray, 1 black*
jumbo scallop oval - *1 light gray*
small oval - *2 black*
small egg (optional) - *2 black, 2 light gray*
medium bow (optional) - *1 any color*
1/4" dot punch - *1 black*
1/8" dot punch (optional)

Trim the two light gray eggs as shown, cut the 1/4" black dot in half, and glue one half to the dark gray circle for a nose (with the round part facing down). Punch two eyes with the 1/8" dot punch, just above the nose, and glue the dark gray circle to the black one. Attach the jumbo scallop oval to the top of the circle just above the eyes with a black oval on each side of the head for ears, and the trimmed light gray eggs to the black eggs. Trim the tips of the black eggs in an inverted "V" to create hooves. Attach the bow at the neck, if desired, and the two hooves at each side of the bow.

Monkey
jumbo balloon - *1 dark brown, 1 black*
medium apple - *1 light brown*
small strawberry - *1 light brown*
1/4" dot punch - *2 dark brown, 1 black*
1/8" dot punch (optional)
small oval - *1 dark brown*

Trim the apple, balloons, strawberry, and the black 1/4" dot as shown. Glue the trimmed apple to the lower narrow section of the dark brown balloon, attach the oval (lengthwise), and add one half of the black 1/4" dot (round part facing up) for the nose. Punch the eyes with the 1/8" dot punch just above the nose. Glue the brown balloon to the black one, the trimmed strawberry to the top of the head, and the two brown 1/4" dots on each side of the head for ears.

Pig
jumbo circle - *2 light pink, 1 black*
5/8" circle - *1 dark pink*
small heart - *2 dark pink*
spiral - *1 light pink*
medium rectangle - *4 light pink*
1/8" dot (optional)
mini scallop flower (optional)
medium bow (optional)

Trim the rounded tops of the hearts slightly, cut a straight slice off one of the jumbo circles, and round off the corners of each rectangle. Glue the dark pink circle on the lower section of the untrimmed jumbo circle, and use the 1/8" dot punch to make the eyes and nostrils as shown in the completed design. Glue the pink jumbo circle over the black one, the small hearts at the top for ears, and attach the head to the trimmed circle. Glue the spiral at the rear for a tail and place the rectangles, vertically and staggered in length, at the lower edge for the feet.

The blue ribbon is optional, but it nicely covers the paper edges that join the head to the body. To make the ribbon, punch a mini flower and a medium bow from blue paper and a 1/8" dot from white paper. Trim one of the ribbons off the bow and attach the flower at the top. Glue the dot in the center of the flower to finish the ribbon.

Giraffe
jumbo balloon - *1 gold, 1 black*
medium apple - *1 gold*
medium snowflake - *1 dark brown*
medium sun - *1 dark brown*
small oval - *2 gold, red*
1/4" dot punch - *4 dark brown*
1/8" dot punch (optional)

Trim the apple, snowflake, and sun as shown. Glue the red oval at the narrow end of the gold balloon, the trimmed apple over the oval, and the trimmed sun at the top of the balloon for hair. Punch the eyes with the 1/8" dot punch just above the nose, and glue the gold balloon onto the black balloon. Glue a gold oval to each side of the head for ears, one section of the snowflake for each horn, one 1/4" dot to the top of each horn, and the other two 1/4" dots to each side of the nose for nostrils. Draw in the details.

Chapter 14

Easy Craft and Gift Ideas

Be creative and expand the use of your paper punches by using them on materials other than paper. For example, make jewelry, charms or buttons by punching shapes from the shrink plastic that is sold in many craft stores. Follow the manufacturer's instructions for sanding, painting and baking the plastic. The jumbo punches work best for this, but some of the medium punches will work as well. Notice in the illustration the actual size of the punched shape before and after baking. You can also use the punches for punching into magnetic sheeting, sticker paper, craft foam sheets, and the super thin sponges that expand when you place them in water.

Keep in mind that you can use any of the designs in this book for projects other than photo memory albums. For example, create greeting cards, invitations, note cards, gift tags, table place cards, bookmarks and seals for your envelopes. You can even make jewelry, magnets, plant pokes, cake decorations, mobiles, garlands, and elaborate framed works of art. See pages 54-55 and page 62 for detailed information on the gift projects below.

punched size

size after baking

jumbo & small maple leaf   jumbo & small oak leaf   jumbo birch leaf   jumbo & mini scallop flower

medium & small tree   medium & small apple   medium & small heart   small & silhouette tulip

jumbo pointed butterfly   duck   running bunny   medium & small rabbit   medium & small bear   cat

medium & small star   pointed & mini star   medium sun   spiral   medium & small foot   jumbo & small balloon

jumbo hand   jumbo, medium & small bow   medium & small snowflake   medium & small train

circles   square   triangle   egg

1/8"

jumbo   5/8"   1/2"   1/4"   1/16"   rectangle   oval   diamond   jumbo bell

strawberry

jumbo & small house   jumbo scallop oval   baby buggy   moon   cloud   birthday cake   baseball player

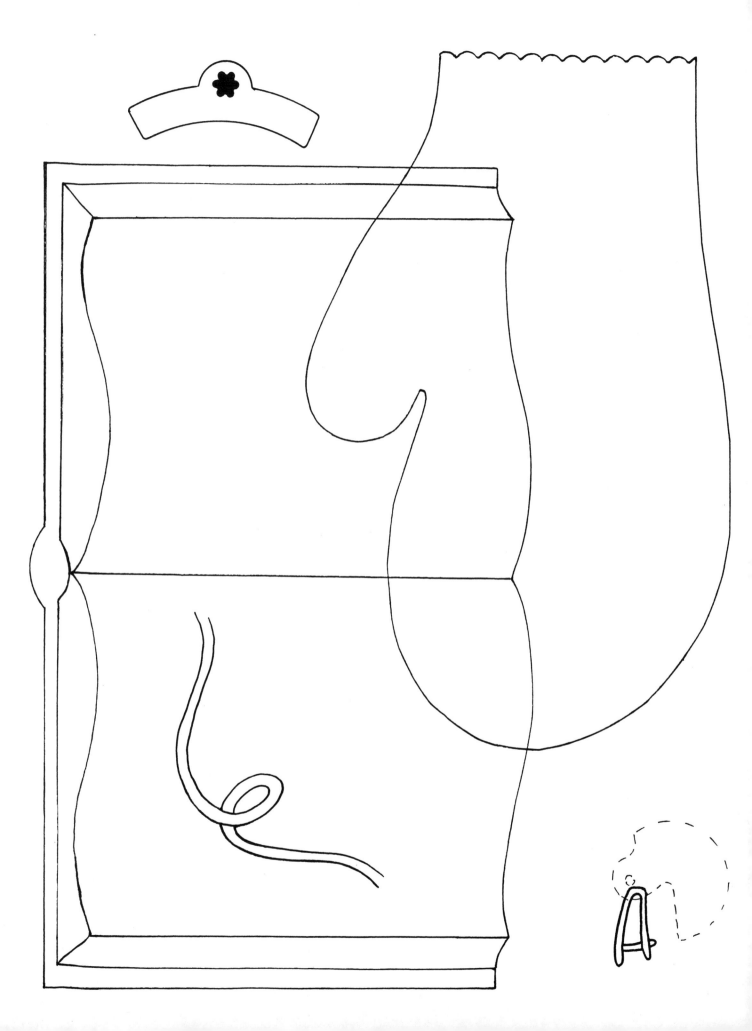

Resources

To order additional copies of *Punch Happy*, send $14.95 plus $2 shipping to

Tracey L. Isidro   or to: Living Vision Press
P.O. Box 522   P.O. Box 326
DeSoto, MO 63020   Bountiful, UT 84011
                                          801-292-6007
                                          www.inconnect.com/~lvision

Also available from Living Vision:

A Lasting Legacy, Scrapbooks and Photo Albums that Touch the Heart by Souzzann Y.H. Carroll. This is a complete guide to creating memory albums that are meaningful, attractive, and made to last and be enjoyed. It offers many practical resources including a list of Top Tips at the end of each chapter to summarize the information and make it easy to find. Over 180 sources of retail and wholesale supplies are included in the resource appendix. The book is 168 pages, 8 in color, and has many illustrations including layout ideas for contemporary and heritage memory book pages. Send $19.95 plus $2 shipping for each copy ordered.

Punch Sources

Online

Eudemodia
www.eudemodia.com
HappyPeople@Eudemodia.com

Sidelines
www.saraslines.com
sara@saraslines.com

Mailorder

Rocky Mountain Crafts
540 E. 500 N.
American Fork, UT 84003-1976
www.rmcraft.com
801-763-8628 800-270-9130
FAX 801-756-0577

Carol Wright Gifts, Dept. LL
340 Applecreek Rd., P.O. Box 8512
Lincoln, NE 68544-8512
402-474-1377
limited selection, good prices on those available

Retail Stores

The Heartland Paper Company
616 West 2600 South
Bountiful, UT 84010
801-294-7166

The Keepsake Garden, Inc.
5129 Lemay Ferry Road
St. Louis, MO 63129
314-892-3887

Punch Manufacturers & Distributors

Fiskars Inc.
7811 W. Stewart Ave.
Wausau, WI 54401
www.fiskars.com
800-950-0203

Family Treasures
24922 Anza Drive, Unit D
Valencia, CA 91355
800-413-2645 FAX 800-891-3520

Marvy-Uchida/Uchida of America, Corp.
3535 Del Amo Blvd.
Torrance, CA 90503
www.uchida.com
800-541-5877 FAX 800-229-7017

McGill, Inc.
131 E. Prairie St.
Marengo, IL 60152
800-982-9884

Adhesive

Adhesive Products, Inc. (API)
520 Cleveland Ave.
Albany, CA 94710
510-526-7616 FAX 510-524-0573
Memory Mount, Crafter's Pick glue

Stamps

Northwoods Rubber Stamp, Inc.
841 Eagle Ridge Lane
Stillwater, MN 55082
612-430-0816 FAX 612-430-0763

Photo Credits:

Author photo by Mark C. Patterson of Fast Foto Studio

Victor Isidro portrait on back cover by Don Bess Studios